"Dan Bernstein's fabulous new book, *He Kept His Day Job*, is presented as a memoir, but at its heart lies a love letter to his lifelong muse. Music tugs at his heart and the readers get to share poignant, wryly humorous, life-affirming experiences through the eyes of a semi-professional musician and the colorful characters encountered at gigs, rehearsals, and even funerals. It's a unique perspective that reminds us all of our humanity, and just how powerful music can be to heal, create community, and spread light and joy in the world. If you don't see yourself somewhere in this book, you're not actually reading it!"

— JOHN JORGENSON
Grammy-winning musician & composer

"This is a wonderful story of a life full of interesting people, entertaining (and funny) experiences, and unexpected growth as a musician and person who pursued his musical avocation in his "spare time." He certainly makes an outstanding case that an individual can participate in and practice an art form throughout their life, adding richness and depth that they might never have imagined when they were young. I thoroughly enjoyed this book and highly recommend it!"

— DAVID CAFFEY
California Jazz Education Hall of Fame; past president of International Association for Jazz Education; board member of International Society of Jazz Arrangers and Composers; Professor Emeritus of Music at the University of Northern Colorado, where he directed the School of Music

"In my view everyone, not just professionals, should connect with their creativity and the joy that brings to one's life. Dan Bernstein illustrates how he's done just that in this heartfelt memoir."

— JUDITH CARMICHAEL
Grammy-nominated jazz pianist; host of podcast/NPR show *Judy Carmichael's Jazz Inspired*

"Dan Bernstein captures the remarkable, border-crossing power of music to touch us all in this moving and entertaining book. A talented wordsmith and versatile musician, Dan shows us the joy and humanity of music through the lens of his colorful life as a student, journalist, and musician. Dan reminds those of us that have dedicated our lives to music of the reasons why we did so in the first place in this touching and witty memoir."

— JEFF HELLMER

Interim Director, Butler School of Music; University Distinguished Teaching Professor, University of Texas at Austin

"Dan Bernstein's memoir is a beautifully written account of the importance of art in the world. Any adult even remotely considering pulling their instrument, paintbrushes or dance shoes out of the closet should read this book. As a professional musician, I was reminded of all the reasons I was so drawn to music in the first place .. Even "Pros" should strive to maintain Dan's "Amateur" level of commitment to Music."

— ALEX ILES

Principal trombonist of the Long Beach Symphony Orchestra, performs or has performed with the LA Philharmonic, Hollywood Bowl Orchestra, LA Chamber Orchestra and jazz groups, including Maynard Ferguson and the Woody Herman Orchestra, Bob Florence's Limited Edition, The Seth McFarlane Orchestra and Gordon Goodwin's Big Phat Band

He Kept His Day Job

FANFARE FOR THE COMMON MUSICIAN

He Kept His Day Job

Fanfare for the Common Musician

Dan Bernstein

FUNNY BONZ PRESS

Published in the United States of America
By Funny Bonz Press
Riverside, California 92506
danbernstein629@gmail.com

Bernstein, Dan
    He Kept His Day Job: Fanfare for the Common Musician

     1. Bernstein, Dan 2. Journalism 3. Whistling 4. Trombone 5. American jazz
I. Title.

ISBN 979-8-88992-657-3

Book design by Beverly Simmons, *ffortissimo* DESIGN
Manufactured in the United States of America.

Set in Minion Pro.

Front cover photo: Dan Bernstein, 2022. *Photo by Carrie Rossema.*
Back cover photo: Dan Bernstein, 1967. *Photo by Roy W. Bassett.*

Contents

Illustrations

Dedication

FOR MY LATE mother, Belle Bernstein, the family's very own Music Woman who knew the territory and merrily marched (and dragged) me into a world I grew to love. Even after a stroke left her unable to talk, my mom gleefully belted out her part in our daily duet, "You Are My Sunshine." And for my late father, Harry Bernstein, who may not have had a musical bone in his body. All he wanted was for my sibs and me to be happy.

FOR MY WIFE, Candia, whose inexhaustible (if tested) patience made this book possible, and whose piercing (if occasionally stabbing) insights made it much better.

Prologue

BACK IN THE summer of 2020, I was packing up to leave a volunteer gig at an assisted-living complex when a gentleman with a snow-white pony tail wheeled up and asked, "How long have you been doing this?" When I said I'd had been playing trombone since grade school, Joe Holder told me he had grown up playing trumpet and flugelhorn in Norfolk, Virginia. After graduating from high school, he decided to become a forester and chase girls, though perhaps not in that order. He put away his trumpet and flugel and never played them again. Then he looked at me and just shook his head. "I've been kicking myself ever since." Joe was ninety. That's a lot of kicking.

Joe is not alone. When I've finished playing a song at a hospital or sometimes after a gig with fellow musicians, people have approached me to offer strikingly similar confessions. "I played piano when I was a kid," they might say. Or trumpet, clarinet, saxophone, flute, violin, guitar. You name it. "But I didn't keep it up and I've regretted it all my life."

Their stories are layered with the unspoken pressures, challenges and choices that shape our lives. But for a few random twists that pinballed me in a different direction, this could have been my story, too. These confessions stayed with me and eventually inspired me to write this memoir in hopes that others might find ways to keep their day jobs and keep their "instrument" – whether it's a paint brush, chisel, garden trowel, *toque blanche*, tap shoes, trumpet or even an accordion – out of the case.

I was a fourth-grader when the music salesman handed me a trombone. It was a consolation prize for a kid who wanted to play clarinet. For a very good reason, the music man turned me down flat and handed me a large brass object notable for its slide and bell. "Try to get a sound out of *this*," he ordered. I huffed and puffed and managed to produce an unsavory blat. The rest is history, unremarkable as it may be.

I played in grade school, kept playing in high school and college, didn't play much at all for a while, but picked up my horn again and started playing during my decades-long career in newspapers (you might have to Google that word), mostly as a columnist. Now I am retired, creeping ever deeper into my seventies and still playing and practicing, something I once loathed and avoided. But what else could a geezer do during a pandemic besides shop early, practice trombone and write the story that follows in these pages?

This is a true story about the frustration, insecurity, flashes of enlightenment, sheer joy and gratification I have felt while making music for little or no money at all. It is a story about collaboration and chemistry, about lessons learned and the humility that goes with it. It will transport readers to rare and exotic climes: a community college band room where I played in a jazz ensemble with many musicians much more talented than I; my living room, furnished with five chairs, old rags to absorb spit and an Old English sheepdog – our official rehearsal mascot – where I learned that in a brass quintet you cannot run and you cannot hide but you can achieve that immensely satisfying "synchronized swing"; Little Rock, Arkansas and Pasadena, where I "marched" at halftime with a rather notorious college band; Carson City, Nevada, the gracious host city of the early whistling contests; Gatsbyesque parties at Manhattan Beach and graduation ceremonies at a Native American high school; and Kaiser Hospital in Riverside, California, where I played in some of the toughest rooms of all: Oncology and ICU.

Even though this is a memoir, it is not (spoiler alert) a wrenching account of bitter conflicts never resolved or majestic obstacles surmounted. Granted, I probably sucked my thumb longer than most kids, became an accomplished worrier and learned to play an instrument frequently associated with pizza delivery. But I loved my parents and they loved me. I wasn't born with a silver spoon, but I had a trombone with a silver bell. And I rarely missed a meal.

As I wrote this story, I began to recall what I had seen and learned first-hand over more than a half-century of playing: Music can be a powerful force, a language that speaks to the soul. It entertains, comforts and distracts us from our deepest troubles. Remember Billy Joel's "Piano Man":[1]

> *It's a pretty good crowd for a Saturday*
> *And the manager gives me a smile*
> *'Cuz he knows that it's me they've been comin' to see*
> *To forget about life for a while*

Music can triumph where mere words fall short. In *The Last Hurrah*, Edwin O'Connor's mid-century political novel set in fictional city much like Boston, the Ninth Ward Democratic Club holds its annual spring dance. There is an orchestra.

> *Music strengthened fraternity; in the benign solvent of a song, traditional animosities faded. Dr. Joseph Brady sang, "My Wild Irish Rose"; Mr. Arthur Piccione sang, "O sole mio"; the applause for the latter nearly equaled that for the former. It was evidence of the growing tolerance of the Irish; it was even greater evidence of the growing numbers of the Italians.*

Is there an elixir out there that actually works wonders? "Music and singing," noted Viet Thanh Nguyen in his novel, *The Sympathizer*, "keep us alive, give us hope. If we can feel, we know we can live."

On Oscar Night 2021, when Jon Batiste clutched his little golden statue for Best Original Score, I almost felt like he was speaking to me.

> God gave us twelve notes. It's the same twelve notes that Duke Ellington had. Bach had. ... Every contribution with music that comes from the Divine into the instruments, into the film, into the minds and hearts and souls of every person who hears it ... the stories that happen when you listen to it and watch

and the stories you share ... the moments you create,
the memories you make. ... Man, it's just so incredibly
special.

Batiste is far more eloquent than I, but we share a soft spot in our hearts for those twelve notes. As he spoke, I found myself thinking: If a supremely gifted African-American artist from Louisiana and a bald Jewish white guy from Denver both see music as a vehicle that transports us to places we might not otherwise visit, if music is the grist for stories, the storehouse of memories and has the power but not necessarily the venom of a spoken language, I might have a story to tell after all.

As you read this brief memoir, you will meet generous, talented and demanding people, including a teacher who habitually slugged me, fairly gently and for good reason, and taught me a squeaky clean word that helped set the tempo for the rest of my life; a substitute tuba player whose unexpected question at the end of a gig changed absolutely everything; a community college professor/director whose soft-spoken leadership and high expectations steered an adult jazz band through difficult music as well as a pandemic; a trumpet player/ scientist on a mission to kill citrus pests before they killed citrus; a trombone player who ultimately had to choose between his inner band geek and tech nerd; and yet another trombone player who tripled as a sheriff's dispatcher and a mom and found a measure of healing in her music after a horrifying tragedy. In short, you will meet people who, like me, juggled their jobs, families and music. And through newspaper columns reprinted in these pages, you will read about people whose lives were enriched by music and people whose love of music may have saved the lives of others.

This story is written for a general audience, including readers who may never have played a note in their lives and parents like my mother who herded her kids into music like a border collie drives sheep to a fresh pasture. It is also for those hardy musicians who have kept their day jobs as well as those who stowed their axes but can't stop thinking about playing again. Much of it was written after I met Joe Holder at that assisted-living place in Sisters, Oregon. When he told me he hadn't stopped kicking himself for abandoning his trumpet and flugelhorn, I realized that could have been me. I put my horn down, too, and probably would have felt the same regret gnawing at my guts if I hadn't picked it back up and brought it along for the ride. Which doesn't mean I have never kicked myself. I still do every time I remember what I once said to the person who shoved me into music in the first place: Belle Bernstein. My mom.

Chapter 1

Yakety Yak (Don't Talk Back)

My mother drove us everywhere: to a little round church on Hampden Avenue that doubled as a summer school for typing lessons; to the YMCA on South Colorado Boulevard so we could learn to swim and save lives; to a downtown Denver movie theater for double-feature operas, filmed in black and white, to prevent us from going blind during a solar eclipse; to music lessons, part of her grand plan to get us into college. There was a stretch when my older sister, Paula, played viola; my younger sister, Debra, played bassoon; and my kid brother, Jeremy, played oboe. Even though she already had a college degree, my mother took up cello. My father took up residence in a sound-proof closet.

Belle Bernstein didn't just drive us. *She drove us. Hard.* I don't remember where we were going the day things got ugly (I was probably in seventh grade), but I do remember she was driving me, hard, to quit whining and keep playing piano and trombone. One thing I didn't know or think to ask was: what was driving my mom? I was the type of kid who assumed their parents' lives began only after they started having children. I wasn't curious about what they had done before I came along because it never occurred to me that they had done anything at all. But with the help of my sisters and brother and Paul Stein, a cousin who had burrowed deeply into what he called an ancestral "rabbit hole," I began to assemble a few pieces to a still-incomplete puzzle. And some things began to make sense.

BELLE SPERLING WAS BORN in Chicago on Christmas Eve 1923, the first of Nathan and Anna Sperling's three daughters. Nathan, whose given name was Naftaly, was born in 1892 in Riga, Latvia, part of the Russian Empire. He had little formal education which probably explains the family tensions that would boil over later. Nathan emigrated to the United States in 1911, figuring that staying home meant he would be drafted to fight in Tsar Nicholas II's army. He knew that most Jews were sent to the front lines. He settled in Chicago, worked in the laundry business (not much more detail than that) and enlisted in the U.S. Army in May 1918. He was promptly sent to Europe and deployed, of course, to the front lines, where he almost immediately got gassed. He came home from World War I and became a naturalized U.S. citizen in July 1918.

Anna Kulwinski was born in Kovna, Lithuania, on Christmas Day 1896. She and her parents arrived in the U.S. in 1898. Her dad was a rabbi, but when they settled in Chicago, he and his relatives worked in the liquor and saloon business. Nathan worked with Anna's brothers, which is probably how they met. They married in March 1923 and my mom, Belle Reva, was born nine months later. By 1927, Belle had two sisters and the family had moved to Seattle. Still suffering from the effects of WW I mustard gas, Nathan desperately needed a climate with more breathable air.

My mom started piano lessons in Seattle, but as my sister, Paula, put it, "sabotaged herself" by learning to play by ear. This left her unable to decode some of the music she really wanted to play. She also joined a choir and would continue to sing in choral groups in high school and beyond. I have vivid memories of my mom decked out in her choir robe in our Denver synagogue, Temple Emanuel.

I don't think my mother ever longed to be a musician, but there was something else she was stubbornly determined to do. Belle Sperling, who grew up in the 1930s during the Great Depression, wanted to go to college. Her father had next to no education and struggled to support the family in various lines of work, from delivering laundry to starting his own Home Roofing and Siding Company after moving to Denver in 1938. But his narrow-gauge vision of upward mobility did not include college, especially for a girl, especially for his first-born daughter, whose "job" was to stay home and help *him* run the family business. Nathan Sperling's opposition to his oldest daughter's desire to attend college became so venomous that it poisoned the relationships between my mother and her two younger sisters. They were daddy's little girls and she wasn't. But she was one tough cookie.

That toughness had been baked in early. She was born with a dislocated hip. The doctors pinned her back together as best they could, but she couldn't walk when she should have been toddling. She grew up with a noticeable limp and the inevitable ridicule and teasing that went with it – even from her sisters. That bad hip helped my mother acquire a scar tissue commonly known as thick skin.

She was a strikingly beautiful young woman. Her senior picture in the 1941 edition of *The Angelus* – Denver's East High School yearbook – reveals only a hint of her rise-and-shine smile.

("*Rise and shine!*" she would sing, mainly on school days, from the top of the stairs that led to my basement bedroom.) More revealing are her eyes, which gaze upward, beyond the lens and toward an unseen horizon. *Her* horizon.

She is also pictured in a group photo of "The A Cappella Choir" and is listed as a member of various clubs.

But the photo that jumps off the page finds her in Row 1 of a club called Junto, whose English translation is "a group of persons joined for a common purpose." The purpose in this case was college.

> *College in all of its puzzling phases interested the members of Junto this year. And so among the guest speakers heard at the club meetings were a professor and some (college) students who spoke about how to make the necessary adjustments to college life.*

My mother would have to make "necessary adjustments" that even Junto could not have foreseen. She graduated from East High and, defying her father, enrolled at the University of Denver in the fall of 1941. Then came Sunday, December 7. Pearl Harbor. By June 1942, with the United States at war with Japan and Germany, Belle Sperling had moved to Eaton Town, New Jersey, where she worked as a drafter and technical writer for the U.S. Signal Corps, a communications branch of the U.S. Army. There she stayed until September 1944. A month later, she enrolled in the University of Michigan's College of Engineering. She is pictured along with twenty-three other somber, business-attired women, in a 1945 UM publication under the heading "Soc-y Women Engineers." She might well have graduated from Michigan and become an electrical engineer. But back home in Denver for the summer of '46, she met a guy who'd recently been discharged from the Army Air Corps. She married Harry Bernstein that November. Between 1948 and 1952, they had four kids, including one who believed he was being subjected to a form of torture that no child should have to bear: taking piano and trombone lessons at the same time.

It was afternoon, after school, and my mom and I were zipping along Interstate 25, approaching the Yale Avenue exit as I complained that my life and spirit were being crushed and sucked dry by the unrelenting pressure of preparing for music lessons. "Preparing," of course, meant "practicing." I hated to practice and was trying to make the case that hating to practice trombone and piano at the same time was too much of a burden for someone who – and here I deftly played my trump card – was also expected to get good grades.

Good grades were the blue-chip stocks in our home. Our parents didn't pay us to bring home As. But if we *did* bring them home, we avoided withering cross-examination. Sometimes, I'd return from school proudly flapping a paper with a large A-minus emblazoned in red across the top. But once the confetti had fallen and balloons had gone flat, my mother would inquire, *"Why didn't you get an A?"* As we reached adulthood, this became an affectionate punch line among us sibs. Our mom laughed right along with us. But when we were kids, *Why Didn't You Get An A?* had the ring of a felony indictment.

That said, Belle Bernstein wasn't always "all in" when it came to advancing our education. In 1951, just after she gave birth to my sister, Debra, *The Rocky Mountain News* ran a story headlined "Salesmen Stay 'Way, Cries Harassed Mother." The harassed mother, identified as "Mrs. Harry Bernstein," was fed up with these leeches who scoured birth announcements, tracked down moms and tried to sell them photos, baby furniture, insurance and, in one case, the definitive version of a nursery rhyme. From the story:

> *There was the woman selling books who told her, "There are 37 versions of 'Mary Had a Little Lamb'" and implied that the child might be damaged for life if the mother didn't buy the book with the correct version.*

My mother opted to raise four damaged children.

DRIVING THE HIGHWAY that day, my mom found herself engaged in an argument with a "musician" who did not like to practice; a slow reader who did not like to read; a sweaty palmed test-taker who scored miserably; and a student who, on Day One of seventh grade, was officially classified as below average. Out of 12 "sections" in our class, I landed in Section 7. My sister, a year ahead of me, perched at the summit in Section 1.

My mother had to be wondering exactly whom she had the pleasure of chauffeuring that afternoon. She swooned over opera, loved the symphony and bought every classical album she could find, provided it was on sale. My older sister couldn't remember a Saturday afternoon when opera didn't pour out of the radio. I remember my mother teaching us words to a song that I later learned was the No. 1 hit for the Jimmy Dorsey Orchestra in 1936. She must have been thirteen or fourteen when she first heard, "Is it True What They Say About Dixie?" Yet, how and why music became one of my mother's life-long passions remains a mystery, perhaps because her four kids never asked. But now here she was, chauffeuring her oldest son – her own flesh and blood – as he begged, pleaded and whined to slash his workload in half. Who was this kid?

Of course, I didn't know her very well, either. I didn't know the woman who was driving me was herself so driven that she defied her father, went to college, dropped out of college because of a war, got married and had kids and *still* trained her gaze on that long horizon. I *did* know she went back to the University of Denver and got her bachelor's degree in accounting in 1959, though what I really remembered about those days were our customary dinners of prunes and potatoes, which the babysitter refused to eat. I had no way of knowing that, in the years to come my mother would get a master's in public administration and a doctorate in Speech Communication. She would become a bank executive in a male-dominated field and, to the tune of "Home on the Range," serenade us with description of her duties: *Organize, Plan and Control, for that is the manager's role.* ... Much later, she would organize, plan and control her own head-hunting business that paired high-priced engineers with oil and gas companies. The five-figure fees she pulled in made our heads spin.

Had I known all this, I still might have spewed my regrettable car-stopper as we argued along the Yale Avenue offramp. But at least I might have foreseen how she would react when I exploded, *"Shut up!"*

I'm sure the words shocked us both. But knowing what I know now – all the teasing, ridicule and resistance that my mom put up with as she cleared one obstacle after another – I suspect that those awful words were little more than flesh wounds. Belle Bernstein remained perfectly composed behind the wheel and, upon coming to a stop at the bottom of the offramp, calmly dropped what she must have regarded as the nuke. "Wait until your father hears about this."

My father had a belt.

Harry Bernstein could lasso horses and break down a Colt .44 revolver, then put it back together again. Fast. When my brother, Jeremy, a witness to these skills, told me what he'd seen, I couldn't square them with the man who rose early each morning to watch *Sunrise Semester* on public television and spent leisurely Sunday mornings in the bathtub, reading. I found myself asking, "Who was this man?"

Harry Simeon Bernstein was born in Grinnell, Iowa, on August 26, 1910. An "Affidavit of Delayed Birth Registration" affirms that he was the first born *and* "Legitimate." His dad, Samuel David Bernstein was the "Owner of Icecream Store." His mom, born Lena Edith Shpall, was a "Housewife." Ice cream. Iowa. Legitimate kid. All the essential ingredients of a Norman Rockwell masterpiece. Except Samuel, twenty-three, and Lena, who may have been older, weren't deeply rooted Iowans. They were Jewish, born in Ukraine, and arrived in the U.S. in 1907. It is not clear whether they knew each other before they left Eastern Europe, but they married in Iowa in May 1909. My dad, Harry, was born fifteen months later. Sam and Lena would move to Colorado and have four more children.

The sparsely filled puzzle of my dad's youth sometimes seems as wide open as the Colorado plains. The family lived in Monte Vista in the southwestern part of the state, where my grandfather started out as a farmer and eventually owned a cattle ranch. My dad and his two brothers cared for the cattle, which meant they had to ride, rope and shoot. My grandmother ran a store in Monte Vista and my dad sometimes helped her out. One day the store was robbed. The suspect got nabbed and went to trial. His defense: "Are you going to believe me or a Jew?" My dad was the only witness. The robber was convicted.

Along with ranching and economic survival, religion and education appeared to be cornerstones of the Bernstein family. The five kids, like their parents, were raised as Orthodox Jews. My dad split time between Monte Vista and Denver, where he went to public high school. His senior yearbook reflects the image of the Harry Bernstein I knew, not the calf-ropin', gun-totin' cattleman, although our dad always took us to Denver's annual stock show, a winter event known for its sub-zero, blizzardy ambiance and thousands of the finest and fattest cattle in the West.

"He possesseth an intellectual mind," reads the inscription below "Bernstein, Harry" in the 1928 North High *Viking* yearbook.

His eyeglasses are notable for their small, dark circular frames. His wavy hair, which had long-since disappeared when we met, sat high atop his otherwise shaved head, foreshadowing the present-day fade. His lips are sensuously thick. His straight-ahead expression is deadly serious, with a remote threat of a grin. He was a member of the Latin Club.

"To a real smart fellow," signed Fannie Janovitz. "Here's to a future lawyer and I'll hire him," wrote Marjorie Cochran. The 1920s were roaring. Babe Ruth hit 60 homers my dad's junior year. Anything must have seemed possible his senior year. But just months after he graduated, the stock market crashed. Although the early 1930s are yet another missing piece of the Harry Bernstein puzzle, it's not a stretch to conclude that my father's plans were sidetracked, if not totally derailed. He didn't receive his bachelor's degree from the University of Denver until 1937: a "liberal arts" degree, with an emphasis in botany. Three years later, in 1940, he earned a master's in accounting. At thirty-one, he tried to enlist, but, he wrote, "Uncle Sam quibbled over one's ability to see and no recruiter would take me." They took him four months after Pearl Harbor, thanks in part to a recommendation from a gentleman who had sold my grandfather some Angus cows just before the 1929 crash. By 1942, that gentleman had become the governor of Colorado.

"*To Whom It May Concern:*" wrote Gov. Ralph Lawrence Carr,

> *I understand that Harry S. Bernstein is making application for officer training. Mr. Bernstein is an upstanding young citizen of Colorado, able and intelligent. I feel sure that he would prove to be an asset to any branch of the service.*[2]

He served in the Army Air Corps as an auditing officer for four years and four days.

On a summer weekend in Denver, soon after his 1946 discharge, he met Belle Sperling. Until then, he had been ticketed to enroll in the University of Chicago's graduate school of economics. But now at age thirty-six, he wrote, "I found myself drifting toward marriage." Four months later, the drift reached its destination: his wedding. My dad had graduated from high school a year before the Great Depression, my mom a year before World War II. For years, both marched to someone else's drummer in the Signal Corps and Air Corps. Even "Greatest Generation" seems short of the mark. This was a selfless generation, teeming with people driven to serve, bum hips or questionable eyesight be damned. But now, Harry and Belle Bernstein began building their own lives – and producing new ones.

Belle and Harry Bernstein on their honeymoon, 1946.
MILLMAR PHOTOS, LAS VEGAS, NEVADA.

BY THE TIME MY mother dropped the nuke at the Yale Avenue offramp, my dad had become the father of four and a CPA. He had also become the lawyer his classmate had envisioned back in 1928. Unlike my mother, he didn't fret about our grades, though he did have a word with Mr. Sorensen when I failed the first six weeks of seventh-grade wood shop. Perhaps because of the topsy-turvy arc of his own early life, my dad often said he just wanted me to be "happy." Music did not sing to him, but philosophy did. So did economic theory. And there was that lasso and that gun. Like many fathers, mine was a complex man. And he did have a belt.

But Harry Bernstein was not a violent man. *"Got dammit the brake!"* he shouted at me one Sunday afternoon just before I hit the back wall of our garage as he was teaching me to drive. That was about as agitated as I ever saw him. Whenever he visited my room, I was usually already in bed. Sometimes, he popped in for a pop quiz. "Four times four!" he'd declare and wait for my answer. Sometimes, he read to me from *Gulliver's Travels*. I fell asleep with images of Lilliputians creeping around in my head. When I grew older, my dad sent me beautiful letters.

But on the evening of the Yale Avenue Offramp Incident, he entered my bedroom with what we called "the strap." His punishments were largely theatrical, always with an element of suspense. He wasn't the type to burst into the room, belt in hand. He entered with an aura of entitlement, making it clear that I had no right of privacy and no place to hide. He slowly unbuckled the belt and gave me every opportunity to watch it slither through the loops of his trousers. The actual administration of justice, however, was half-hearted, for the mighty strap carried the sting of overcooked linguine. He wasn't out to maim me. He just wanted me to feel like scum for talking to my mother that way. In this, he succeeded magnificently. I apologized to him, to her. I was truly sorry and remorseful. I would disappoint my mother again and again, but those words would never again be hurled in her direction.

Yet, I must point out for the record that, shortly after the Yale Avenue incident, I was allowed to stop taking piano lessons. I still balked at the thought of practicing my trombone, but I had run out of excuses. And I couldn't help thinking that my mom now had me exactly where she wanted me.

Chapter 2

Long, Long Ago

If my mother actually did hatch a grand scheme to launch us into college on the wings of unusual musical instruments, she must have known from the start that none of us would take flight on the common piano. But she also knew there was no better launching pad than our ancient upright which suffered through at least one coat of black paint and cruel and unusual punishment during practice sessions.

Mrs. Hortense Zuckerman was the one piano teacher I have never forgotten. She had a beautiful singing voice, a no-nonsense aura that frightened students like me into paying attention and a small bald spot. Thanks to her and other piano teachers, I learned important fundamentals, such as what a "note" was and how one note differed from another. I learned about octaves and scales, measures and chords, eighth notes and *dotted* notes, flats and sharps. I learned the difference between black keys and white keys, treble clef and bass clef and how to play music with both hands at the same time.

I once played a two-handed song called "Long, Long Ago" before a friendly audience of other students and parents, including mine. Though I got stuck in a few places, I managed to escape from the jam and finish the tune. If that recital was the highlight of my piano career (it was), fourth grade was the first movement of what would become the theme and variations of my musical life. Fourth-graders, it seemed, had reached a critical stage in human development: We were able to hold a musical instrument in our hands and even put it in or press it against our mouths. But before we could even dream of doing something like that, we had to master the tonette.

There is no evidence[3] that Ziegner Swanson of the Chicago Musical Instrument Company was known as the "Father of the Tonette," even though he is credited with inventing it in 1938. It became a popular instrument designed to gauge student interest without bankrupting parents. It enabled aspiring musicians to experience the thrill, power, magic and portability of performing such crowd pleasers as "Three Blind Mice" and "Twinkle, Twinkle Little Star." The tonette was a gateway instrument that could lead to a lifelong dependence on brass or wind instruments, reeds or mouthpieces and (for innocent bystanders) earplugs. The tonette itself was a shiny black plastic tube that from various angles resembled a large slug or a small submarine. The business end of a tonette was flat and looked like a whistle. The idea was to blow air through the whistle while fingers covered and uncovered the holes in the tube to produce a recognizable crowd pleaser.

Tonette "lessons" were less formal and far less intimidating than piano lessons, primarily because the tonette was not a piano. I can't even remember my tonette teacher, although I'm sure there was one. I recall taking group lessons, relying on fingering charts to learn which tonette holes had to be covered to produce a melody. We also learned what happened when our fingers failed to completely cover those holes. "Fingernails On Chalkboard" was definitely not a crowd pleaser.

One evening near the end of my Tonette Period, I found myself in someone's house with a bunch of other kids, including my best friend, David Mesch. This, I realized much later, was the tonette virtuosos' equivalent of a Tupperware Party. Or a commencement ceremony. This was the night we would finally hold the instrument of our dreams in our own tonette-tested hands. But had I known the Michael Neri story, I would have understood right then and there that not all dreams come true.

Neri was once a Philadelphia kid who longed to play trombone. But the music man said no because his arms were too short. There was no way he could reach the instrument's seventh and ridiculously far-away position. Fine, said Neri, I'd like to play the cornet. No problem, said the obliging, if devious, music man, who presented him with a clarinet, for which he developed an instant hatred. By the time we met, Dr. Neri had risen to the top job at Kaiser Hospital in Riverside, California. But in a way, life had literally short-changed him. He never got to play the trombone.

Well before we arrived at the Tupperware Party, David Mesch dreamed about playing the saxophone. This became my dream, too. But the man who brought the instruments didn't bring a sax. He explained that aspiring fourth-grade sax players should first learn to play the lighter, less complicated and (a nod to the parents) cheaper instrument that faintly resembled a tonette. David and I decided we wanted to play clarinet.

We had much in common. Our dads were lawyers. We lived on the same street and went to the same school. But there was a key difference. David's mouth did not house an "appliance" designed to discourage him from sucking his thumb. I had him there. This wire gadget featured barbed prongs that would puncture any thumb that dared to enter any mouth. How the presence of this dental version of cyclone-fencing became known on Tupperware night I don't recall. My own mother might have mentioned it, though probably not in a boastful way. But once it got out, the man with the instruments made it clear that he was not about to let some kid insert a perfectly good clarinet mouthpiece into his razor-wired mouth.

But he wasn't about to let me walk away empty-handed, either. He was a businessman with a job to do: get musical instruments into the hands of little kids so their parents would feel obligated to rent perchance to buy. With this in mind, he snapped open a case whose velvet-lined interior cradled something that appeared to require some assembly. Within a minute or so, he had attached a curved piece of pipe with a large funnel on one end, to a U-shaped piece of pipe that he said was "locked" and should stay that way. Finally, he twisted a silvery mouthpiece into a hole at one end of that U-shaped pipe and handed me the entire contraption. Just like that, I was holding a trombone.

"Try to get a sound out of *this*," he said, directing me to a door that led to a garage.

Before my mom and I left that house that night, I discovered (a) I *could* get a sound out of a trombone, and (b) unlike clarinets and trumpets and all the other instruments the music man brought with him, only the trombone was meant to be played in a garage.

CHAPTER 3

Roll Over, Beethoven

I STARTED TROMBONE lessons with Mr. Ellman, a soft-spoken man with a melodious baritone voice. Each week, we sat in a small room at a Denver music store where Mr. Ellman instructed, encouraged and corrected with all the force of a teddy bear. I learned all seven trombone slide positions even though I could barely reach the sixth. I learned that the same note could be played in different positions, thereby saving wear and tear on several joints I would need a few decades later. It occurred to me that an even better approach would have been to decrease the length of the trombone slide and assign each note just one position, putting them all within easy reach of just about any kid. I don't recall discussing this with Mr. Ellman.

Mr. Ellman had meaty lips, so whenever he demonstrated how the trombone should be played, his heavy silver-plated mouthpiece excavated a deep, circular imprint on his mouth. Years later, my wife would diagnose this condition "trombone mouth," not meant to be a term of endearment. To me, this lingering disfigurement represented hard work and dedication. But as a young musician of the Sixties, I couldn't help observing that guitar players, who displayed no apparent symptoms of guitar mouth, attracted a disproportionate share of shrieking females. Though the term had yet to be coined, I sensed that "trombone mouth" might be a social liability. I also began to suspect that the trombone wasn't just an instrument. It was also a punchline, with a nickname that suggested it had been custom-designed for a sewage treatment plant, not a band.

"How are you coming along on the old slush pump?" some would ask when they saw me lugging my trombone. If the music man who dashed my hopes of playing clarinet had said, "Take this slush pump into the garage," I wouldn't have touched it. Indeed, the trombone has traveled a potholed path in search of its identity and respectability. As recently as 2022, a female friend lovingly called it "chick repellent."

The first trombones may have been sighted in the early 1400s in northern Italy.[4] Or southern France. Or both. Or neither. Maybe Germany. Even though the instrument itself had arrived, nobody could decide what to call it. *Trombone* was definitely in the mix, but so was *tuba grossa*, which was Latin for *large trumpet*. The Italians may actually have coined the word *trombone* by merging *tromba* (trumpet) with *one* (large) as early as 1439. But did that settle it? Of course not. In the beginning … which happened to be during the Renaissance, the trombone resembled a shady character with a long list of aliases: *trombone, tuba grossa, trumpet, trompette de menestrels* (trumpet of the minstrels) and *posaune*. The French were so *je ne sais quoi* about trombone that they assigned the same word to the instrument and the paperclip. Easily the most unfortunate word associated with the trombone was *sackbut*, which of course made early trombone players the sackbuts of most Renaissance jokes. By the late 20th century, American trombonists were widely portrayed as either delusional (Definition of an optimist? A trombone player with a pager) or virtually unemployable, especially as a musician (How do you improve the aerodynamics of a trombonist's car? Remove the Domino's Pizza sign from the roof.)

In tenth or eleventh grade, I started taking lessons from Tasso Harris, a well-known (though not to me), tough-love professional who someone must have mentioned to my mother. I had graduated from an easy-on-the-parental wallet student trombone to a beautiful, I'm-not-worthy King 3-B Silver Sonic that remains the only piece of silver my wife and I own. I remember begging my parents for a baseball mitt autographed by Mickey Mantle, but pining for King 3-B? No recollection whatsoever. The Silver Sonic snuggled into a cushy "coffin" case that must have weighed close to a ton. Each week, I trudged to the bus stop, trombone in tow, and climbed aboard the No. 8 which shuttled me and my coffin from Southeast Denver to downtown, where I walked to an old red-stone building that might originally have been an apartment house. I let myself in through an obscure, unwelcoming back door and descended the stairs that opened onto a spacious, luxury-deficient, cave-like studio.

Tasso, whom I never addressed as "Tasso," was dashingly handsome, with silver streaks racing through his jet-black hair. His dark eyes did not flare with delight or high expectation when I stepped into his line of vision. They seemed dulled with resignation that I was likely to disappoint him. Again. If I'd been more inquisitive and less intimidated, I might have discovered that Mr. Harris set such high musical standards because he lived by them and knew what living by them could accomplish.

Tasso had been playing in clarinetist Artie Shaw's jazz band when the Japanese attacked Pearl Harbor. A year later, word got out that the sailors in the South Pacific longed for the "hot jazz" they'd left behind. Shaw, who had enlisted in the Navy and served on a minesweeper, received new orders: form a band. He did it partly by rounding up some of his old buddies who had also joined the Navy. Tasso was one of them. The "501" performed in jungles and on ship decks, often under a splotchy sky of military camouflage.[5]

Harris also played with drummer Gene Krupa and in groups that backed touring musicians, including Elvis Presley when he swiveled through Colorado. By the time I sat down for my first lesson in his cave, Mr. Harris had either led or soon would lead the University of Denver's jazz band to championships in state and national competitions.

Mr. Harris assigned me exercises and etudes designed to improve my technique, breathing and tone. "Song style," he wrote on my music. He meant play it like you'd sing it. The trombone is what Goldilocks would have grabbed if her daring daylight break-in had been motivated by a search for the perfect brass instrument: not a trumpet (too high), not a tuba (too low). The trombone was just right. Like its low-strung cousin, the cello, the trombone is often singled out as the instrument whose tone and range resemble the human voice when it stops talking and starts singing. Sometimes, I would surprise both of us by actually playing "song style." When I fell short, Mr. Harris slugged me on my right knee.

Goldilocks's choice. CARTOON BY PHILIP NEUMAN.

It was only a glancing blow, not at all painful. More of a corrective than a punishment. Still, a slug to the knee is a slug to the knee. I don't want to leave you with the impression that every lesson was a contact sport. Sometimes, Mr. Harris would just sigh, "Bring me a note from the doctor stating you are feeble-minded." With such documentation in hand, he promised to tailor his teaching to my dimness. Sometimes, he actually complimented me. "You played that less lousy than you played it before." But my overall impression is that, more often than not, I let Mr. Harris down.

Oddly, he had the opposite effect on me: He helped me grow up. One Saturday morning, an hour or two before a scheduled lesson, I telephoned Mr. Harris and told him a lie. I can't remember exactly what it was, but it was designed to cleverly mask the real reason I had to cancel my lesson: I wasn't prepared. I hadn't practiced. When I finished my heart-rending story, Mr. Harris, who assumed my father also was a veteran, simply said, "Ask your dad what T.S. means." And hung up. I had a feeling I knew what "T.S." meant, so I didn't bother to ask my dad. Mr. Harris had seen right through me. Though I didn't think it through in these exact terms, I realized that lying my way out of a self-inflicted predicament fooled no one, including myself. It would have been much better to apologize for the short notice, explain that I hadn't practiced and assure him that I'd find a way to pay him for the time he had set aside for me. But not many teenagers think this way. It would have been best to have practiced in the first place, hopped aboard the No. 8 and made a valiant attempt to play song style without getting slugged.

Small as I felt that day, Mr. Harris could make me feel like a late-blooming genius. One day, as we discussed the pros and cons of Mouthpiece A versus Mouthpiece B, Mr. Harris asked which I preferred. My first thought was that it was a trick question, that Mr. Harris already knew the answer and was just waiting to see if I'd get it right. The problem was, I didn't know which mouthpiece I preferred because I had only tried one of them. But did that really matter if Mr. Harris already knew the answer? I felt trapped. Finally, with maximum trepidation, I said, "I don't know. I think I'd like to try the other mouthpiece first." If there had been a brass band in the studio, Mr. Harris would have cued it to play a fanfare. Or, if he had one handy, passed me a Mensa membership card. Instead, he just said, "That's one of the smartest things I've ever heard you say." For once, I hadn't let him down. I could have missed the No. 8 and floated home.

The teachers I remember are those who taught me something I've never forgotten, even if it had nothing to do with the subject they happened to be teaching. Even if I had disappointed them time and again. This time, I hadn't disappointed Mr. Harris for something I'd done, but for something I had failed to do. Because no one, including Mr. Harris, had told me to do it.

After I explained this to him, he grabbed a piece of paper and a pencil and began to scribble. "Do you know what this means?" Mr. Harris asked, showing me a word crafted in deliberately large print for the benefit of the feeble-minded. It means, he explained, that there are certain things you do even if nobody has mentioned, suggested, assigned or ordered you to do them. You do them because they need to be done and you know it. You do them because you, or someone else, will be better off if you make the effort.

He handed me the piece of paper, which I soon lost or tossed. But that one word carried an electrifying jolt. Countless times, it has spurred me to act even though no one has said or whispered a thing. Because it never hurts to show a little "initiative."

Even after Mr. Harris introduced me to that live-action word, I was not a model trombone student. Though I dutifully took lessons that my parents encouraged and paid for, I didn't look forward to them. Trombone lessons were not isolated events. They were the culmination of a week or, in my case, a weak of practice. My big sister Paula, easily the family's most dedicated musician, spent hours playing her viola in front of a mirror in a bathroom whose acoustics rivaled the restrooms in Carnegie Hall. I found practicing tedious, frustrating and discouraging. Most of the time, the sounds I produced were tortured or gravely wounded. I couldn't stand listening to myself.

But much as I hated to practice, I loved to perform. Even though I became sweaty palmed and nervous, I had a competitive streak that motivated me to enter solo contests and audition for city and statewide groups. Results were mixed. "Lovely sound," wrote one solo-contest judge, after I'd played "Among the Sycamores" in junior high. Four lines later, he added, "frightfully flat." But at least I was *playing*, not practicing. And playing a lot. I played in my high-school band that was chock full of flutes, trumpets, clarinets, saxes, French horns and tubas. I didn't have words for it back then, but I felt comfortable and confident – the priceless dividends from the sense of belonging. We were young, raw and at least one of us was frequently frightfully flat, but we sat in band class and made music together and eventually *performed* it to please ourselves and an audience. After every concert that my sibs or I played, my parents drove us to our favorite coffee shop and treated us to ice cream sundaes. For me, the entire performance package, from the downbeat to the ice cream, proved fabulously addictive.

At times, I thought my trombone had been specifically manufactured to belt out brassy marches: "Mr. Touchdown," "On Wisconsin!" and "Fight On!" I couldn't play loud enough at our high school football games. But when I played my first-ever jazz solo in a ballad called "The Nearness of You," I had to have been thinking "song style." And when we expanded to an orchestra, with violins, violas and cellos and timpani, there was an entirely different sound, with entirely different music. Here we were, gawky teenagers playing classics written by long-dead composers who had probably never set foot in America. It excited and amazed me that we high schoolers could produce music that sounded (remotely) similar to the notes that wafted out of the radio or my mother's massive collection of vinyl.

One particular composition always made me smile, which made it difficult to play the trombone. It premiered a few years before I entered high school – 1829, to be exact – and was actually an overture to an opera. We rehearsed it for weeks, maybe even longer, and for much of that time I was doing what brass players frequently do in orchestras: Nothing. Playing trombone in an orchestra is like standing in a check-out line behind six shoppers whose carts are stuffed with enough groceries to last six months. But it was usually worth the wait. I knew I'd be playing when it really counted. I also knew that the piece we had been working up would thrill my unsuspecting classmates – and me.

Attendance was mandatory for my high school's student assemblies, which was okay because student assemblies usually pre-preempted classes that no one liked anyway. These assemblies didn't last long, maybe forty-five minutes. But it might have felt like a three-day detention as the captive Thomas Jefferson High School audience surveyed the sea of violins, violas, cellos, flutes and clarinets. Not an electric guitar in sight. The orchestra's trumpets and trombones might as well have hung "NOT IN SERVICE" placards from their bells for all the time we had to just sit there and count rests. But I was excited. I knew what was coming.

I panned the audience as we played our final number – the overture to that opera – and saw students squirm as if they had been invaded by red ants. Others seemed to have nodded off and had likely begun to drool. The way I saw it, it was all part of the plan. The orchestra plodded ahead with gooey flourishes suitable for napping. Even a brief and furious flare-up involving us brass players only served to remind the rudely awakened snoozers where they were. Then, at last, the trumpets shattered the calm with a familiar Saturday morning, black-and-white-TV fanfare. In my mind, the entire concert had been a setup for this moment. Suddenly awake and alert, my classmates returned to those "thrilling days of yesteryear" as the orchestra galloped to what was widely known as the theme song of *The Lone Ranger*. I was supposed to be playing. I *was* playing and trying hard not to smile. But I could see that the audience was giving us a second look. There was a buzz. There were random bursts of laughter, revealing delight and surprise. After we'd finished Mr. Rossini's *William Tell Overture*, waves of applause and cheers cascaded toward the stage. I felt the chill and the goose bumps that went with it. Once again, I had gotten to play my trombone and perform for an audience. I loved every second, including the waiting.

Thomas Jefferson's instrumental music program might not have been as robust as some, but in addition to the concert band and the orchestra, we had pit bands for school musicals and a brown-and-gold-uniformed band for football games. And of course, there was the jazz band. Once I began playing the old slush pump, I gradually became aware of just how beautiful and versatile this instrument really was. Not by playing it, of course, but by listening to the living-room record player whose first allegiance was to my mother's classical music. But Tommy Dorsey made an occasional cameo with "Song of India" or "I'm Getting Sentimental Over You." Glenn Miller served up his satiny "Moonlight Serenade." Carl Fontana and Frank Rosolino dropped by. There was something about jazz that got under my skin. It was upbeat and skipped along with unpredictable rhythms and harmonies that could flow with syrupy warmth, then quickly cool to nail-biting jitters. Jazz sounded fresh, prepared that day, that instant. Created perhaps never to be *re-created*, which was just fine because with every new second came a new idea. My admiration of jazz far surpassed my ability to actually play it. I wasn't a star in our jazz band. The few solos I played were written out. But I was a cog in a school stage band, which once produced a bit of off-stage drama.

It was a Friday night in May 1962. I was thirteen and I had a gig. The next day, I had an even bigger gig: my bar mitzvah. I was home alone, cooking my own dinner – a greasy hamburger that kept spitting at me – because the rest of my family had gone to Friday night services at our synagogue. Normally, we spent Friday nights at home. We lit the Shabbat candles, sang a blessing or two and sat down to dinner. At least that's what we did until the night my dad backed into a candle and caught fire. My mom quickly extinguished the blaze, my dad was unhurt though his shirt was ruined. We prudently retired the candles.

My parents had gone to temple that evening because their attendance was expected as part of the run-up to my big day. But I stayed behind because this bar-mitzvah-eve service conflicted with a school jazz-band concert. If my dad and mom had sung from the same prayer book, I probably would have gone to services. But my dad was raised Orthodox and although my mom's father almost certainly was an Orthodox Jew, it is unlikely that she and her sisters grew up in a religious household. Nathan Sperling had narrow ideas about what women and daughters should do and strict adherence to religion and ritual evidently did not make the list. My dad and mom seemed to have struck a deal: They would have a religious household, but that religion would be Reform Judaism, which was not nearly as strict as Orthodox.

When I told the band director I couldn't make the jazz concert, Mr. Lallo appealed directly to my mother, who would have been a helicopter mom even if there were no such thing as helicopters. I was rooting for him all the way. I *wanted* to play that concert. Mr. Lallo managed to convince her that Friday night services could get along fine without me, but the Thomas Jefferson stage band definitely could not. If my parents debated the matter, I was out of the loop and had no mixed feelings as I stood alone in the small kitchen of our modest, single-story brick home. (My brother and I had basement bedrooms with window wells that became late-night, cat-on-mouse crime scenes.)

After I ate my burger, I walked to my nearby high school and played in the jazz band. The next morning, I read from the Torah and delivered an uplifting speech in a falsetto voice. Moments after I had completed my ceremonial exit from the sanctuary, my mom burst through the doors and shouted, "Danny! You were wonderful!" My dad, who had spent months helping me prepare for this big day, put his arm around me and gave me his warmest, proudest smile. He might not have said much, but words weren't necessary. That smile meant the world to me. The hybrid weekend of jazz and Judaism had been a triumph. Days later, like all newly minted bar mitzvah boys, I began to thank the people who had showered me with gifts. Writing thank-you notes was a mandatory bar-mitzvah-boy ritual and a perfectly valid excuse to avoid practicing my trombone.

AT THE SUGGESTION of Mr. Lallo and with the ironclad support of my mother, I auditioned for all-city and all-state bands and orchestras, which led to my memorable acquaintances with C. J. Shibly and Ludwig van Beethoven. C. J. attended George Washington, which, like Thomas Jefferson, was one of Denver's newest public high schools. We were both in the Class of 1967. Sometimes, I auditioned well enough to play first trombone. Most of the time, C. J. or someone else occupied that seat mainly because they were better players. Of the two of us, only C. J. would later tour the world as a member of the Glenn Miller Orchestra and play in bands that backed Tony Bennett, Carol Channing and Mel Tormé. When his days on the road ended, he returned to Colorado and became a band director.

C. J. was confident and proficient in that first-trombone chair. But when the music stopped, a gleam of mischief stole into his hang-dog eyes. If trumpet players are the swaggering jet pilots of the brass section, trombone players are known to be the shrewd subversives – or comical and lazy, depending on your Internet search. C. J. paired his mischievous eyes with a Tubby-the-Tuba laugh, making him bi-polar in the very best sense: He took music seriously but kept things light and loose.

During one orchestra rehearsal, the conductor stopped everything and zeroed in on the trombone section. We were having a tough time with a difficult passage and by the third or fourth time through, one of us still was not quite getting it. It happened that he also was playing a brand-new, blindingly shiny bass trombone. The conductor became increasingly impatient. You could see it in his pinched face and hear it in his slow-boil voice. As the tension ticked upward, the poor guy with the new horn grew more tentative, afraid to make a mistake. Which guaranteed that he *would* make a mistake. C. J., who was playing first trombone, may have felt it was his responsibility to *do something*. Or maybe the random thought just popped into his head. Whatever the motivation, he leaned toward our embattled mate and, in a stage whisper that could have been mistaken for an airport public address announcement, said: "You should have bought a boat!" Everyone within earshot, including the guy with the new trombone, crumpled into laughter, crumpling the tension right along with it. C. J. had a sly way of making a point: Music was supposed to be challenging, but not stifling. Otherwise, the joy of playing and performing would be choked off – certainly not the best strategy for anyone aspiring to entertain an audience. Even high school musicians yearned to entertain because it was exhilarating. But it was not without risk and anxiety.

Beethoven was a familiar name to me. Like zillions of others, I could sing the first four notes of his famous Fifth Symphony: *Da-Da-Da-Duh.* Four beats to open the Fifth Symphony must have driven the purists crazy. One of the many things I didn't know about Beethoven was that his Fifth Symphony was a watershed moment for trombones: First performed in 1808, it was the earliest symphony – or at least the earliest symphony still performed to this day – to include trombones. Before that, the old slush pumpers were relegated to church and opera gigs. Trombone players were probably deliriously grateful to Beethoven until they realized that admission to the symphony club came at a steep price. Emphasis on steep.

The last movement of the Fifth requires the first trombone player to nail a high C, which is not exactly a cinch, but doable. But that's just the warm-up. A little later, Ludwig writes in a high F, still the "highest note for trombone in standard orchestral repertoire."[6] To put this high F in perspective, there are three perfectly suitable lower Fs at a trombone player's disposal. This made the need to climb yet another octave highly questionable, at least from a trombone player's vantage point, which was looking straight up. Reaching that highest F is akin to conquering Mt. Everest without a rope, oxygen or even a smart phone. Beethoven was asking a high school student in Denver's all-city orchestra to just suck it up and hang a high F. Since Denver was a mile-high city, whoever selected this piece probably reasoned the trombone player had a head start. But the trombone player, who happened to me, harbored grave doubts.

"Think you can hang your high F?" the French horn player in front of me kept asking as the concert drew closer. How did I know? I don't recall exactly how I trained for the big moment, but I was a teenager so I suspect I trained like a teenager climbs steps: several at a time or in this case, eight at once. I'd play the easiest F, then leap to the next highest F, then close my eyes, take a deep breath, jam the mouthpiece to my lips and hope to nail the highest F with a clear, pure tone while leaving the top of my head intact. (I later learned there were far better ways to reach this summit, but they required practice.)

Though I was a New York Yankees fan by this time, I had yet to hear Yogi Berra's analysis of baseball: "Ninety-percent of the game is half mental." Still, I sensed there was a powerful state-of-mind component to the Beethoven Challenge. To ease unneeded pressure, I holed-up in our living room and listened to the symphony over and over again, hoping the dreaded F and I would become better acquainted. The more I listened, the more I realized that when the highest F finally appeared on the page, Beethoven's Fifth was galloping into the home stretch and the conductor had taken the whip to the entire orchestra. Assuming I could hang it, I figured my high F would be barely audible because everyone else would be wailing away beneath it. I began to realize Beethoven had been kind enough to provide the Trombones of 1808 (and me) with an orchestral safety net. Which is how I talked myself down to a state of only moderate anxiety that, at crunch time, allowed me to just suck it up and hang that high F and earn a quick wink from the horn player. Well before I was old enough to vote or drink, my trombone and I had reached the point where there was nowhere to go but down.

CHAPTER 4

Pomp & Circumstance

"POMP & CIRCUMSTANCE" was among the six military marches on the playlist for the 1902 coronation of King Edward VII of England. Edward Elgar, an Englishman with a lush handlebar mustache, composed the pieces and borrowed the title from his countryman, William Shakespeare. From *Othello* (Act III, Scene 3):

> *Farewell the neighing steed and the shrill trump,*
> *The spirit-stirring drum, th' ear-piercing fife,*
> *The royal banner and all quality,*
> *Pride, pomp, and circumstance of glorious war!*

"Shrill trump." Shakespeare had no idea.

The "Pomp & Circumstance" we've come to know arrived in America in 1906 when Elgar received an honorary degree from Yale. It was played as he walked off the stage, degree in hand. Perhaps because of its "regal melody, warm tone colors and stately tempo,"[7] this march became a graduation staple. The instruments Elgar called for included three trombones. On a June evening in 1967, I sat in a trombone section that numbered considerably more than the Elgar trio. I was a senior and could have walked with my class in the University of Denver arena, but felt I had a duty to be with the band. I also felt much better off than my fellow grads, whose sole duty was to just sit there until they were summoned to receive their walking papers. If there was any downside to playing "Pomp & Circumstance" in a stately tempo, it was playing it again. And again. And again. And again. And again, until the

stateliness threatened to decay into a limp dirge. But we played stately-
ish until the last diploma was handed to the final graduate in a class
that exceeded 500. When Mr. Lallo finally lowered his baton my career
as a high-school trombone player came to an end.

THERE WAS NEVER a question that I would go to college. It was a given.
It took me much too long to realize that what seemed inevitable to
me was either unattainable, undesirable, unaffordable or just plain
unheard of for others.

By 1967, President Kennedy had been dead four years. The fight
for civil rights had become bloody and deadly. Martin Luther King Jr.
and Robert F. Kennedy were assassinated within months of each other
in 1968, my freshman year in college. The Vietnam War, in which some
of my high school classmates fought and at least one died, was ripping
the country apart. Every 18-year-old male had to register for the draft.
Most college men received 2-S student deferments that immunized
them from military service. I was not one of them. When I turned 18,
my mom and I drove to the non-nondescript office that housed my
draft board. I presented a doctor's note documenting my long history
of asthma, (not feeble mindedness). Unlike my father, who had tried,
failed and kept trying to join up during World War II, I was relieved to
receive my military classification: 1-Y. Unfit to serve barring a national
emergency. A year or two later, with no prompting or petitioning
that I know of, I was re-classified 4-F. Unfit to serve. Period. I don't
remember feeling a great sense of relief because if there was never a
question that I would go to college, there was very little worry that
I'd be going to Vietnam. I was a white, middle-class college kid with
asthma. I wouldn't fight in the war, but I would march against it. I
would also march in a college band. At halftime. This was my America.

I HAD FALLEN IN LOVE with the cover. Exotic splashes of red-tile roofs,
swabs of palm trees. California! A place I'd never seen, except on TV
and on the cover of this particular college catalogue. I knew Stanford
University had an excellent reputation and that the odds of getting
accepted were quite long. But I applied anyway. The worst thing they
could do was reject me, which is exactly what they did. My grades were
good enough. But my SATs swirled down the test-score toilet. I scored
well south of 600 in math and English. The Stanford admissions folks

must have rolled their eyes in are-you-kidding-me unison. Instead of departing for the land of red-tile roofs and palm trees, I headed south to Colorado Springs – a ninety-minute bus ride from my Denver home, my parents and their washing machine.

Colorado College was intimate and challenging. It offered small classes and caring, accessible professors. The sting of Stanford's rejection had dulled when I arrived for freshman orientation. I settled into the dorm room, which my mother had disinfected with Pine-Sol and which I shared with a friend who had finished up high school in Iran. I was excited, yet homesick. And intimidated by my fellow freshmen who had devoured every book on the summer reading list. I hadn't come close.

I decided to major in political science for a simple reason: Politics and politicians fascinated me. I had gotten hooked in the summer of 1960 as I stared at our basement TV, watching Lyndon Johnson and John Kennedy fight for the presidential nomination at the Democratic National Convention in Los Angeles. I was eleven. Now, seven years later, with no interest in or aptitude for real science, I fancied myself as a *political* scientist, which in those days was really a student of political history. But a total academic nerd I was not.

I pledged and de-pledged a fraternity, joined the debate team (faring rather poorly) and went out for baseball (faring even worse). Colorado College was small enough that a student could try just about anything except, in my case, ice hockey.

I found time to write a sports column for the college paper. I'd written a similar column for my high school paper even though my English teachers were not entirely captivated by my compositions. *"Needs transition!"* frequently found a home between the paragraphs of my essays. *"Wordy!"* became the one-word plug they stuffed into to my irrepressible geysers. *"Good!"* showed up just often enough to keep me going.

As a reader, I was the opposite of voracious. I once crammed for a high-school test on *Moby Dick* by reading the Classics comic book version the night before the exam. My grade accurately reflected my effort. But I was a sucker for a laugh. Art Buchwald, whose *New York Times* column appeared in the *Denver Post*, showed me that humor was a powerful delivery system for a serious message. Stan Freberg and his occasionally searing but hilarious record album, *Stan Freberg*

Presents the United States of America, planted the seeds of satire into the shallows of my brain. Alan Sherman's lyrics opened my ears to yet another potent delivery system: musical parody.

Long before writing high school essays and sports columns, I began experimenting with the lowest form of humor as I recapped baseball scores for a neighborhood weekly: *Acme Painting splattered Bell Plumbing 10-2; Graham's Landscaping edged Goldberg's Deli 3-2.* These were not actually printed in the *University Park News*, but merely examples of what I used to write. They didn't call me the next Hemingway for nothing – or ever.

Needs transition!

I grew comfortable and confident with my classes at Colorado College. With Tasso Harris's word lodged deep inside of me, I took the initiative to study without waiting for anyone to tell me. Because, I quickly realized, nobody cared.

One thing I cannot recall doing at Colorado College is playing my trombone, although I came across a letter I'd sent my parents mentioning I was in a jazz band. It is possible that starting a new life as a college freshman and living on my own (except for laundry runs to Denver), I didn't have that much time for trombone. What I clearly remember is returning to my dorm room after Christmas break. It was a Sunday night and I was making my bed and talking to E. J. Connor, a Chicago kid who'd become a good friend. As we talked, I was honestly *shocked* to realize that the first semester of my freshman year in college had flown by so quickly. Standing there, amid blankets and sheets, it dawned on me that more than just a semester had disappeared. It was time, life itself. I knew I was powerless to stop it, but I had to do something more than just stand there and watch. It was time to make a move.

CHAPTER 5

Suite: Judy Blue Eyes

THE SECRET PLAN I'd hatched months earlier had actually worked. Now, I was savoring my first taste of California: the billowy skirts atop the beanpole palm trees, the ancient, inviting red-tile roofs. But as I escorted myself on a leisurely tour of sites I'd only seen in pictures, I began to feel increasingly small and lonely.

No one except Paula, my big sister, knew that I had once again applied to Stanford. I had decided to keep it on the down low in case I failed again. I wasn't unhappy at Colorado College; I was just itching to get out of Colorado. I could do my own laundry. Paula had taught me how to iron my shirts. What other skills did I need? The world was at my doorstep. Well, maybe not the world, but California was a short plane flight away. I'd never been on an airplane.

My mom was thrilled when I broke the news that Stanford had accepted me. My dad, however, was subdued and worried. He'd always told us he didn't care what we did as long as we were happy. He thought I was happy and comfortable at Colorado College, and he wasn't wrong. He thought that planting myself in a faraway state, at a much larger school, as a transfer student who didn't know anyone would be a jarring change. He wasn't wrong about that, either. But a restless teenager, I was more like my mom. "What can happen?" she'd ask when facing a challenge, whether it was going back to school time and again or starting her own business. As I grew older, I became the worrier my dad would have understood. But on September 13, 1968, dressed in my best slacks, an ironed white shirt, a conservative narrow tie and blazer, I soared above a layer of whipped cream clouds into the deep blue yonder. My trombone, safely tucked into its cushy coffin, mingled with my co-passengers' luggage. My first plane flight at last. I was nineteen.

I arrived on a Friday afternoon, all dressed up with no place to live. Transfer students were wait-listed for campus housing. I rented a room in Menlo Park, the next city over. My commute would be a short but treacherous bike ride along El Camino Real. I pictured my dad shaking his head, imagining the direst replies to "What can happen?" Classes wouldn't start for weeks. For me, it was another year, another orientation. At some point, I mentioned to someone who knew his way around the campus that I played trombone. He told me about a band that rehearsed in a shack.

I MUST HAVE looked like an entry-level burglar, casing a joint in broad daylight, as I circled the rundown, one-story shack (or, as I would soon learn, "shak"). It was hiding in a neighborhood of buildings that could have been laboratories, classrooms or entire departments. This weathered former home of the ROTC (Reserve Officers Training Corps) was easy to locate because even before I saw it, I heard rumors of music. Toots, blasts and a trumpet sprinting up a scale while a tuba excavated its way to the Equator.

As I debated whether to walk in or skulk away, a stocky guy with a meek blonde mustache and gentle eyes asked if I needed help. At least a dozen answers leaped to mind, but I gave Phil Imming the short version: I play trombone. It was as if I'd whispered the secret password. We went inside. The cave-like shak was packed with ancient wooden chairs and decorated with patriotic slogans ("Beat Cal") and other people's (mainly taxpayers') property. The overall theme seemed to be Retro Maintenance Yard – a random and impressive array of abandoned or stolen street and traffic signs. The image of a large, black-on-yellow, diamond-shaped "Open Trench" trophy found a permanent home in my brain, which, I admit, reveals a bit too much about my brain. A greatly enlarged replica of a Budweiser beer label completely covered an interior door.

I had heard of the Stanford band, but had never seen it perform and had no idea how to join. I assumed I would have to audition, a thought that made me queasy. But the thought of spending the next year as a commuting hermit made me nauseous. Phil was a year or two ahead of me, played sousaphone and arranged some tunes for the band. He introduced me to a few people, including the lead trombone player and with that, I became a member of "The one, the only, the incomparable Leland Stanford Junior University Marching Band."

I received a friendly welcome into this all-male club that numbered well over one hundred and performed with the Dollies, the official name of the Stanford cheerleaders. Timm Williams, a proud, likable and PR-savvy Yurok Indian who christened himself Prince Lightfoot, also performed with the band. Outfitted in a flowing feathered headdress, war paint, bangles and beads, he danced on the field at football games. Stanford had been the "Indians" since 1930. Prince Lightfoot had been dancing since 1952. At one point, he had his own TV show. But the team's name, the dancing prince and the exclusive fraternity of male instrumentalists were on an invisible but relentless clock. Time was running out.

It was a "marching" band that didn't take the word seriously, which was fine with me. True, we entered a stadium to a military cadence anchored by Larry Gulberg, the charismatic bass drummer who doubled as the heartbeat of the band. But hard as we tried, our ranks gradually came to resemble lazily undulating worms. We extended the simulated marching to our first on-field formation, usually an ax. But once we finished a song, we awaited the drum major's whistle. Whereupon we scattered like startled roaches to our next formation.

LSJUMB bass drummer, Larry Gulberg, 1971. Courtesy Stanford University Archives

The trombone section numbered in the high teens, probably even more, and was led by a senior who had lungs the size of the Hindenburg. He was easy to hear, even on the floor of a sold-out stadium. He also played the right notes. That was one thing I discovered about the band: Playing the right notes the right way was critically important. The only way we could hope to get away with everything else, including halftime shows about sex, birth control and other topics that preoccupied the student body (especially band members), was to be scrupulously careful about our music.

Leland Stanford Junior University Marching Band in "PILL?" formation.
Courtesy Stanford University Archives

The tune that mattered most, even to us, began before kickoff and started with a boiling drum roll. Ever so gradually, it diminished to a simmer, finally evaporating to nothing and taking the crowd noise with it. The band's best trumpet player then pierced the silence with a clear, brilliant and familiar melody. No one sang along, even though the words played on every spectator's lips. As if sneaking through a side door, the band eventually crept in to give proof through the night that the flag was still there. By the end, the entire band had reached its fullest, explosive volume, accompanied by the timely report of a cannon. This arrangement was first performed by the Stanford band in November 1963, days after the assassination of President Kennedy. Arthur P. Barnes arranged this version of "The Star-Spangled Banner" at Fresno State University and brought it to Stanford where he earned his Ph.D. and joined the faculty.

It is unlikely that Dr. Barnes, a slender, soft-spoken counterpoint to the chaos that surrounded him, ever set out to become the soul of the Stanford Band. But his arrangements shaped the band's musical identity. His formula might have seemed simple, but it required unique talent. He arranged music that kids, including Stanford students, listened to on their radios and stereos. He supplied the band with a throbbing repertoire of rock, soul, Motown and pop. In 1971, we recorded an album featuring Dr. Barnes's arrangements of "Hair," "Back in the USSR," "Suite: Judy Blue Eyes," "Woodstock," "Glass Onion" and "Savoy Truffle."

A lot of this music was not *my* music. Rock 'n' Soul didn't get much air play in a family that once sped up a Passover seder to watch Herb Alpert & the Tijuana Brass. My rock 'n' roll immersion occurred mainly during joy rides with my high school friends. I got swept up in Beatlemania, of course, and even temporarily allowed my hair to expand well beyond its normal growth limits so I could fit in with my classmates. I grooved to the lyrics and falsetto of the Beach Boys, but having never actually stepped onto a beach or personally ogled a little surfer girl, didn't completely bond with them. But when Herman's Hermits came along, I couldn't stop singing "Mrs. Brown, You've Got a Lovely Daughter" in a terrible British accent. I whistled the theme to "The Good, the Bad and the Ugly," sang along to "Scarborough Fair" and "Mrs. Robinson" and counted myself among the legions of fans of my fellow Coloradoan, Judy Collins.

But I hadn't heard of "Dock of the Bay," "I Heard It Through the Grapevine" and many other tunes until they passed out the music in the band shak. Once I learned them, practically memorized them and played them over and over again at rallies and games, I felt like I owned them. Listening to that Stanford Band vinyl fifty years later, I was struck by how very much in sync Arthur Barnes was with us and our audience as he churned out hit after mimeographed hit. When he completed an arrangement, he showed up to guide us through it. Then he quietly stepped away. This was a student-run band. Our job was to get his music, now *our* music, ready to perform.

Soon after Phil invited me to join the band, I received my uniform: red blazer and a white hat with a red band. They might have thrown in the black pants, too. I was responsible for the tie. Not long after my first rehearsal, I "marched" into Stanford stadium for the first football game of the 1968–69 season against the San Jose State Spartans. The stadium was filled with jovial fans, confident of victory. I was excited, but nervous. Scattering presented a walk-and-chew-gum challenge: I had to sprint into position without losing my music, which was held in place by the weak jaws of the lyre attached to my trombone. But after a few uneventful scatters, I relaxed into playing my first pre-game show. Until I spotted a bare-legged, helmeted warrior brandishing a sword as he taunted Prince Lightfoot. I was pretty sure the San Jose State Spartan mascot was not welcome on the field at this particular time, but I had no idea what to do about it.

It quickly became apparent that the band had contingency plans for just this kind of situation. Still playing, but peeking out of the corner of an eye, I saw several band mates break ranks, swarm the mighty Spartan and relieve him of his helmet, shield, sword and every other article that could be easily and tastefully stripped away. This was my first introduction to LSJUMB 101: Tradition and Protocol.

LSJUMB 101 also included a rousing display of crowd-pleasing literacy, commonly instigated by the above-mentioned Mr. Gulberg. In crisply articulated unison, band members chanted: *"L-E-L-A-N-D-S-T-A-N-F-O-R-D-J-U-N-I-O-R-U-N-I-V-E-R-S-I-T-Y,"* capped off with *"Organized! 1891!"* The unwritten primer also instructed that we had a special relationship with the UCLA band most likely because we shared a common enemy: the tightly-wound, hoity-toity USC Trojan marchers, affectionately known as the "Rubber Band." But feared and detested as USC was, I learned that Stanford's bitterest athletic rival was UC Berkeley. Stanford and Cal settled things each year in a traditional gridiron clash with a uniquely dull name: "Big Game."

The Friday night before my first Big Game, the band bused to San Francisco, where we snaked through the city that separated the two universities. It was an exuberant, raucous night that began in Union Square and proceeded through Chinatown along Grant Avenue. It was a chilly night and getting colder as we emerged from Chinatown and reached North Beach, home of The City's famous topless bars. Slick, well-dressed barkers paced the sidewalk, enticing and cajoling everyone to step inside and sample the entertainment. Though I didn't accept the invitation, I stood outside and tried my best to leer.

But even the sights of North Beach in the flesh failed to warm me up. My trombone felt like an icicle; my fingers were going numb. We had been "rallying" for hours and I started to shiver beneath my sweaty red blazer. At last, we arrived at a darkened spot and waited for the buses. A few of us stood around a manhole that was exhaling a comforting cloud of steam. As I luxuriated in this unexpected warmth, I realized that the gentleman standing beside me was not a fellow bandsman, but a gentleman of the street who had probably been suffering much more than any of us. As we stood side by side, I also began to realize that part of the warmth I was savoring was being furnished by the robust stream of urine the gentleman beside me was depositing on my pant leg. During the trip back to Palo Alto, in a comfortably heated bus, I began to smell very much like a trombone player with urine-soaked pants. My fingers, however, were no longer numb. And I was able to stretch out a little because no one sat too close to me.

THE BAND DIDN'T travel much in those days. Two trips to SoCal – one for football, one for basketball. In the decades that followed, the band seemed to travel everywhere until asked to never return. But in September 1970, we got itchy. Stanford's football team had blossomed into a contender and our quarterback, Jim Plunkett, was, as the sports writers say, "in the conversation" about the Heisman Trophy. College football and TV brass were well aware of this and had scheduled a nationally televised game between Stanford and the Arkansas Razorbacks. Despite all the chatter, there was no official talk of sending the band to Little Rock. So, sixty-seven of us decided to just meet there.

My summer job as an office boy at a Denver law firm had ended. I flew back to California for my senior year and carpooled to Arkansas with Gulberg, a sax player from San Carlos, a trombone buddy who lived in Fresno and at least one, maybe two, other guys. We ignored speed limits, passed slower cars as if we were immortal and didn't even think about staying in motels. This was strictly a shoe-string, drive-straight-through operation. Little Rock had graciously arranged to put us up in a high school gym. They even provided cots. Somehow, the governor got wind of this and decided this was not his idea of Southern hospitality. The next day, we were moved to a military base. When not rehearsing, some bandsmen toured the city late at night and managed to tweak a drive-in marquee that touted a double feature, including *1,000 Rifles*, and the familiar gridiron call to arms: "Beat Stanford." Soon, the marquee warned passersby that, "Stanford Has 1,000 Rifles." We practiced hard, learning a new piece of music that we hoped would wow the Arkansas fans. We also had a surprise under our belts.

Bandsmen demonstrating the patented LSJUMB scattering technique.
Courtesy Stanford University Archives.

Our mission, in addition to cheering the football team to glorious victory, was to introduce our audience to our version of California culture. To this end, we "marched" onto the field and dropped our pants to reveal a wide and colorful assortment of surfing shorts. Then we played a splashy Beach Boys medley. We also debuted our arrangement of "Suite Judy Blue Eyes," a Crosby, Stills & Nash hit that was getting lots of air time. It was a terrific piece of music. I fell in love with it every time we played it. Later in the game, which Stanford would win, word whipped through the band that Stephen Stills had sent a telegram: "Thank you for playing my song."

The Stanford Band was my drug of choice, a great escape and outright fun to play at football and basketball games (the latter in the much smaller Red Vest band), entertaining stressed-out nerds, campus radicals and buttoned-down alums. But when the music stopped, there was work to be done. I was a disciplined student who pulled just one all-nighter in three years. Rather than procrastinate, I took (you guessed it) the initiative and carefully budgeted my time. This allowed me to write for the college paper, dabble in radio and hold down jobs – washing dishes and waiting tables in a women's dorm, doing odd jobs for an elderly woman and even umpiring softball games. I also worked as a "reproduction technician," which may conjure images of the Free Love Sixties, but actually involved copying documents and blueprints for a company in Mountain View. These gigs, along with scholarships, low-interest loans and my parents' support, got me through school. I had a plan: graduate in political science and journalism, work for a newspaper for one year, then go to law school.

Studying at Stanford often was like living in a snow globe without the snow. No matter how vigorously outside events tilted and shook this globe, the red-tile roofs continued to bake in the sunshine. Palm trees swayed peacefully and undisturbed. But years at Stanford were years of war. People my age got drafted, wounded and killed, making it impossible to live in total ivory-tower bliss.

Vietnam drew me to marches in San Francisco and campus protests that Santa Clara County Sheriff's deputies dispersed with bullhorns and tear gas. I squirmed along with many others as Eldridge Cleaver, an early leader of the Black Panther Party, delivered an eye-opening and occasionally blistering speech to his large private-school audience.

"Although you'd expect him to be extremely radical," I wrote to my parents in October 1968, *"he was really quite moderate compared to what I was looking for. He was also pretty obscene in some parts, which*

was intended, as he said, to 'ruffle some of the girls' Victorian feathers.'" I listened on edge as a leader of the Brown Berets dressed us down while his uniformed, stone-faced brethren worked their way up and down the aisles like church deacons, passing the collection plate, all but daring us to leave it empty. These speeches and the campus-protest stories I wrote for the *Stanford Daily* helped convince me that some things just weren't right. Change was in the air.

When, in May 1970, campus unrest provoked Gov. Ronald Reagan to close the state's public universities and colleges, it was not at all surprising that the Stanford Band scattered to the front lines of protest in complete solidarity with the most hard-core student radicals. Actually, that would have been *extremely* surprising. In fact, some band members immediately beefed-up security in case suddenly liberated members of the Cal band sneaked into Palo Alto under the cover of darkness and tried to break into the shak. Which is to say the band didn't necessarily embrace *every* change – including a move to admit women to our all-male domain. Had campus anthropologists gently probed my views on the matter, I would have been immediately classified (pardon the technical jargon) as a "Male Chauvinist Pig."

Part of the band "culture" included cheers, chants and songs layered with sophisticated bathroom humor and high-quality juvenile sexual innuendo. Most of us feared that female band members would stifle the rankest creativity in our ranks. And though I didn't know it, I was on track to share a prestigious trophy (an empty beer bottle) with a fellow trombone player as the band's "Most Subtle Gross Yeller" for the 1970 football season. It was in this spirit, that I joined the majority that opposed admitting women to the band. My girlfriend, who had already viewed me as a dangerously hopeless "Women's Lib" reclamation project, dragged me by my knuckles to the nearest woodshed where she reduced my arguments (and me) to pulp. "Are you saying that women who played in their high school bands should not be allowed to play in the college band – *because they are women?*" Naturally, I invoked the Fifth Amendment. In 1972, the same year said girlfriend, Candia Young, and I got married, women finally joined the band. Fears of any chilling effect proved to be half-baked and unwarranted. Dr. Barnes had supported the integration all along and predicted the women would "be even brassier than you guys."[8] By all accounts, he turned out to be right.

That same year, Stanford dumped "Indians" and "Prince Lightfoot." The Dollies stopped dancing with a single feather protruding from their heads. It was a controversial move, with the Yurok tribe arguing the name actually honored Native Americans and gave the public a glimpse of their culture. But others, including Stanford's growing population of Native American students, saw nothing particularly honorable about the name "Indians" and the stereotypical and downright crude caricatures that were produced and sold to promote the school's brand. They regarded Prince Lightfoot's own performances in which he placed hexes on Stanford opponents, as degrading, demeaning and flat-out silly. I don't know if these students ever saw or knew about that Stanford Band album, which included a photo of the dancing Prince Lightfoot. The vinyl also included a couple of tunes with titles that aged rather poorly: "Redskin" and "The Scalp Song."

Timm Williams, aka *Prince Lightfoot, 1971.*
Courtesy Stanford University Archives

Once everything had been sorted and squeezed out, "Indians" gave way to "Cardinal," Timm Williams ("Prince Lightfoot") was forced off the field and the Stanford Tree – a dancing human being in a tall tree costume – became the school's mascot. Decades later, a Stanford student and member of the Miwok tribe became the first Native American to don the tree suit and dance along the gridiron. [9]

Jim Plunkett won the Heisman Trophy in 1970, nosing out a quarterback from Notre Dame. I was taking an editorial writing class and penned a brief tribute that John Hulteng, my inspiring and tolerant professor, did not dismiss as entirely frivolous.

> *Jim Plunkett has won from Joe Theisman*
> *The coveted trophy of Heisman.*
> *Success more sublime*
> *Than a PR man's rhyme*
> *Convincingly swayed football's wise men.*

Plunkett had had a sensational year, as did the entire team. For the first time since a 1952 loss to Illinois, Stanford was headed to the Rose Bowl. The band was, too. It was 1971, my senior year. I couldn't think of a better way to leave the ranks of the LSJUMB.

We stayed on the UCLA campus, as did the crisp, proper and positively uptight Ohio State University marching band. To demonstrate our respect and admiration, we gathered at their dormitory and performed a rousing concert. It was a 'round-midnight performance and dorm room lights flickered on in apparent appreciation. We also bused to Anaheim and played at Disneyland. To commemorate my first visit to the Magic Kingdom, I paid an artist for a souvenir caricature. He drew me in profile, holding forth behind a speaker's lectern as a freshly baked pie zeroed in on my larger-than-life nose.

On New Year's Day 1971, we were up early and standing in "formation" in Pasadena. The Rose Parade route covered 5.5 miles, but the most critical point for Stanford's image and ours (which were not necessarily in harmony) was the spot along Colorado Boulevard where the TV cameras put parade participants on full display. My memory is that under the gaze of a national audience, including countless millions treating hangovers, we met the moment. We played clearly and tightly and we "marched" in ranks that, while not perfectly straight, suggested that we weren't treating hangovers. Once beyond camera range, we began to have fun. Between songs, we broke ranks and headed to the sidewalks, shaking hands with spectators as if we were running for office instead of ambling down the famous boulevard on New Year's Day. It was a long parade. But because arthritis, bulging discs and various joints destined for replacement were still decades away, it seemed like a cake walk. Just a long warm-up to the main event: the game itself.

The Rose Bowl swallowed up 102,000 people and welcomed the three key elements to their annual New Year's Day appointments: gentle sun, boundless blue sky and snow-capped mountains. I remember feeling dwarfed by the crowd, awestruck and excited to be standing on the springy Rose Bowl turf instead of slouching at home on a couch.

We sat fairly low in the stands, near a part of the bowl that began to swerve toward an end zone. But it didn't matter. We were packed into the Rose Bowl on the first and best day of the year. Our halftime show had been carefully vetted by athletic department officials who had become accustomed to fearing the worst. They needn't have worried. Our drum major suited up in a flimsy sash emblazoned "1971" and a roomy diaper supported by just one pin. A newborn in a new year.

LSJUMB drum major, Geordie Lawry, at the Rose Bowl, January 1, 1971.
COURTESY STANFORD UNIVERSITY ARCHIVES

I had alerted friends and relatives to scour their TV screens for a bandsman wielding a trombone and wearing a floor mop, dyed bright orange. (I had donned a similar wig – and a *skirt* – for a junior high talent show in which I sang, "I Enjoy Being a Girl.")

We played "Yellow River," a hit song of the day, evidently inspired by the vision of a shell-shocked confederate soldier returning home after the Civil War. The song had morphed into a Vietnam song but our Rose Bowl show, conceived by an informal group of bandsmen known as the Stanford Marching Unit Thinkers (SMUT), flowed in an apolitical direction. We waded into "Yellow River" after forming what had been described to our athletic department minders as a "job shack." However, on the floor of the Rose Bowl and on TV screens everywhere, the "shack" bore a striking resemblance to an outhouse.

Stanford was not expected to win, making the victory all the more exhilarating. After the game ended, a crowd enveloped the band and the entire mass soon was shrouded in a dusky mist or fog that made a joyful atmosphere more intimate. We put on a spontaneous concert, featuring the songs that Dr. Barnes and others had written for us, knowing these tunes were exactly what we wanted to play and exactly what our audience wanted to hear.

In decades since that Rose Bowl, my last football game with the band, I've occasionally been asked if I was the trombone player who got knocked to the ground at the end of a Big Game that saw Cal score a crazy, game-winning touchdown in what became known as "The Play." In fact, that bizarre finale occurred more than a decade later, in 1982. By that time, I was in Riverside, California, beginning my thirty-two-year career as a columnist for the *Press-Enterprise*.

Chapter 6

Nice Work If You Can Get It

I HAD RACKED up enough credits to graduate by early spring, so instead of cap-and-gowning it with the Class of '71, I hopped aboard the Old Boys' Network Express, destination: Salem, Oregon. The state's capital city accommodated two family-owned daily newspapers in one grungy downtown building. *The Oregon Statesman* was the morning paper, the *Capital Journal* the p.m. Both had typewriters.

When I thought about working for a newspaper before going before going to law school, Oregon wasn't in the picture. But a roommate hailed from Salem and his dad, a lawyer, represented the *Capital Journal*. I went up for an interview and Jim Welch, the managing editor, hired me. I started that June while Candia stayed at Stanford to pick up a master's in education. A year later, the day of the Watergate break-in, a burglary that super-charged the newspaper career of another Bernstein, Candia Young married her dishwasher. We had met in her dorm.

We were perfectly matched. Candia was an army brat who had lived all over the world; my childhood travels had taken me all the way from Denver to Cheyenne to visit my cousin. I loved to whistle; Candia could whistle just one note, which turned out to be the *only* note that would register with our wayward sheepdogs. In my most memorable Cub Scout softball season, I either walked or struck out in every at bat except in the last game when I connected for a two-bagger and was promptly doubled off of second base; classmates at the all-girl Catholic high school in Dallas dubbed my future wife "no-bat-Candia." She received a bachelor's degree in mathematics; "math skills," in my case, was a cruel oxymoron. I was a writer; Candia was the best editor I ever had.

The Capital Journal was owned by the Mainwarings, a respected Salem family whose teetotaling matriarch banned food-page recipes calling for alcohol and was not amused when a top editor boarded a fishing boat to produce a feature, photo included, about a topless "baitress." I hired on as a reporter, but also took dictation from the paper's part-time correspondents who provided the granular community coverage that dailies offered back then. I wrote a wide range of stories, including a series about miserable migrant housing in the fertile Willamette Valley. Our photo of a small boy whose large, black eyes welled with innocence said more than my words could have ever hoped to convey.

Dan Bernstein straight outta college, 1972. Author's collection.

Some *Stanford Daily* pals had landed at big papers, including the *New York Times*. I envied them, but my remote outpost brimmed with opportunity to do things large papers would not have allowed me to do. I also did things the paper definitely did not want me to do and things I should not have done.

I became the city hall reporter and wrote editorial page commentaries critical of the people I covered. Reflecting on that dual role of reporter/commentator makes me cringe. I wrote for a journalism review (they were popping up across the country) and took potshots at my own paper. When a labor union organized the newsroom, I was all in.

After a couple of years at the *CJ*, I wanted to make a move. A terrible test score eliminated law school. But my own actions helped me chart a new course. In early 1974, I got fired for making personal long-distance calls on the company dime. Overnight, Candia, who had landed a job as a junior high math teacher, was the sole breadwinner. Embarrassed, lonely and drawing unemployment. I soon received a call from Oregon's folksy state treasurer who was running for governor. (The editor who canned me kept trying to find me a job.) After Bob Straub won the Democratic primary, he didn't need me anymore, if he ever did. But the short gig writing speeches and researching renewable energy pulled me out of my funk, which might have been the idea all along. I returned to journalism.

THERE WAS A $300 potted ficus, extensive change orders to the executive director's bathroom and other extravagant purchases likely to infuriate Oregon taxpayers. I had spotted these juicy items as the only reporter for Northwest News Service, which I co-founded with the *Capital Journal* editorial page editor who'd encouraged me to write those opinion pieces. I had a basement desk in the Oregon Capitol Building. In baseball lingo, my mission was to "hit 'em where they ain't": cover largely ignored state agencies, those dense bureaucracies that subsisted on a rich diet of taxpayer generosity. Each week, I wrote a story that shed some light on these largely faceless operations, made copies, stuffed envelopes and sent them to twenty Oregon weeklies and dailies, including the *Capital Journal*. When it became clear that my subscriber list had peaked, I began asking, yet again, "What's next?"

In the spring of 1976, the *Press-Enterprise* became the only newspaper that answered a job-wanted ad ("Young, bright and aggressive!") I'd placed in a national trade magazine. The paper invited me down for a three-day tryout. The little I knew about Riverside, California, pertained to smog and lots of it. I had actually passed up a chance to meet a P-E editor who visited Stanford on a recruiting mission. But now, I was in no position to be snooty.

I was welcomed to my Riverside audition by young reporters who advised: *If you get a job offer, say you'll cover anything except cops and business.* Over three days, I rewrote "the beekeeper story" – a hot mess of "journalism" regularly served to job candidates – and navigated my way to a neighboring county, where I retrieved a document just minutes before the courthouse closed for the day. Day three found me in the office of Norman Cherniss, the short, pipe-puffing, seemingly humorless executive editor, whom I had yet to meet. (II'd met Tim Hays, the newspaper's owner, as we stood side by side, staring straight ahead, in the men's room.)

When I told him why I'd "left" the *Capital Journal*, Cherniss, who had obviously spoken to someone at the paper, said he hoped I had gotten that out of my system. When he offered me a job, I replied that I preferred not to cover cops or business. Cherniss slid a scrap of paper across his desk, informing me how much I'd make per week, adding, "You'll be covering business."

I returned to Salem in a quandary. Just a few days before I left for Riverside, Columbia University had admitted me to its graduate school of journalism, triggering exhilarating visions of a year in the Big Apple, including frequent visits to Yankee Stadium. Now, I had to make a decision: Take the job? Or spend a year at Columbia and take my chances?

Candia had fallen in love with Oregon. "Does Riverside have trees?" she asked, with a desperate note of hope in her voice. I could only remember the smog, which made it difficult for me to sell the place. But when I called Columbia for advice, trees and smog never came up. "*We* can't guarantee you a job," said a gentleman who seemed quite familiar – and impressed – with "Tim and Norman's little paper" in Riverside. That settled it.

On June, 1, 1976, I started work in a newsroom crowded with long islands of gun-metal gray desks. Reporters sat next to and across from each other, unavoidably eavesdropping on each other's phone conversations and inhaling each other's cigarette smoke. The newsroom climate was a blend of gossip, competition, friendship and insecurity among young reporters who viewed the *Press-Enterprise* as a stepping stone.

At various times, I sat near a reporter who had a pet French fry hooked to a leash by a paper clip; a reporter who fabricated details in a story about a proposed amusement park, hoping his ideas would catch on; a "girl reporter," derisively dubbed by a Riverside mayor thoroughly unequipped to handle a bright, relentless female journalist; and a blatantly nosy reporter who scoured reporters' desks and computer files. He eventually moved to Washington, became a lawyer and went into politics.

These were also some of the hardest-working reporters and best writers I've ever met. For many of them, the paper was a stepping stone. In the first decade or two I was there, many colleagues left for the *Los Angeles Times, San Diego Union, Sacramento Bee* and other larger, respected publications. In the later decades, as the Internet, Craig's List, hedge funds and other predators hollowed out American newspapers, many of my colleagues simply left journalism for PR jobs.

To MY SURPRISE, the business beat overflowed with fascinating stories about what made the city, county and the SoCal region tick: employers large and small, products ranging from sheets of aluminum to RVs to minuscule electronic components essential to just about everything, including military aircraft. The beat introduced readers to "Mr. Milt," whom I accompanied on a pre-dawn trip to the sprawling Los Angeles produce market where he ordered enough lettuce, tomatoes, onions to supply the chain of supermarkets in his territory. I met Jane Walton, owner of the downtown lingerie shop my mom cleaned out whenever she visited Riverside. Jane was the key source for my blockbuster feature about the difficulties men encounter when shopping for brassieres.

After a year, I moved to the county beat and a bureaucracy as ripe with stories as those Oregon state agencies. By 1978, it was on to politics, covering local elections and that legendary California tax revolt, Proposition 13. I kept an eye on the Mission Inn, now a luxurious, historic treasure, but at the time a distressed property owned by the city and overseen by prominent, well-meaning and largely clueless citizens when it came to running a hotel. The board chairman, bemoaning the public's perception of the place, once admonished his colleagues (as I took notes), "We can't make it seem like we're riding a dead horse and going down with the ship." The quotation turned up in the pages of *The New Yorker* under the headline, "Block that metaphor!"

The *Press-Enterprise* – "Tim and Norman's little paper" – was, indeed, a small but clear-eyed, family-owned beacon of American journalism. Tim Hays, a Harvard law grad and special FBI agent during World War II, became editor in 1949 and transformed the paper into the most reliable source of local news in a county the size of Massachusetts. Soon after Hays took over, he hired Norman Cherniss to run the editorial page. In 1968, the *Press-Enterprise* won the Pulitzer Prize Gold Medal for Meritorious Public Service for articles and editorials about white, paternalistic, crooked "conservators" who stole money from the Agua Caliente Indians in the desert. In the 1980s, the *Press-Enterprise* won two First Amendment rulings from the U.S. Supreme Court, giving the public and press the constitutional right to witness jury selection and preliminary hearings.

In 1982, after six years as a *Press-Enterprise* reporter, I became an editorial writer. There were just two us: me and Joel Blain, a self-proclaimed mumbler who, at least in the newsroom, made the Sphinx look like a social butterfly. He was also funny and brilliant. I felt like an academician, ensconced in a tower for two. I had found a home on the editorial page. But one day, the paper's popular local columnist went to work for a start-up called *USA Today* and urged me to apply for his old job. After I submitted a few samples, Norman Cherniss summoned me to his office. He sounded like a man battling severe indigestion, "We'll give this a try," he moaned. "If it doesn't work out, we'll try to find something else for you." In September 1982, after laboring far too long over my debut column, I finally hit the emergency-red "SEND" button on the keyboard that had replaced my typewriter. Joel Blain, who happened to be standing over my shoulder, said, "That's one."

I was thirty-three and had no idea what I was doing. I had walked in cold, drenched in reminders that I had "big shoes to fill." Not long before "That's One" saw print, Cherniss presented me with a collection of "how-to" columns by some of the best in the business. Richard Cohen of the *Washington Post* wrote about New York's Jimmy Breslin and Chicago's Mike Royko, who had "been the ruin of more young columnists than booze or drugs." Because they all tried to write like Breslin or Royko. Fearing the same would happen to him, Cohen stopped reading those two guys. My *Broyko* turned out to be a humor-writing genius named Dave Barry. I stopped reading him. I'm fairly certain he hadn't started reading me.

Jack Smith of the *Los Angeles Times* advised me to procure a trash barrel. His standards were so high that most ideas that arrived via self-serving press releases immediately landed in *his* trash barrel. Which was *never* to be emptied. "Faced with a deadline, desperate for a subject . . . I have dumped my garbage on the floor and groveled on my hands and knees for that precious little piece of paper that I've thrown away."

Bill Safire, a *New York Times* columnist, advised rookies to, "Specialize in being a generalist . . . versatility is all." I took this to heart, providing readers with riveting columns about Riverside's "speed humps," only to switch gears and inform them about my wife's newest power tool or the sheriff's bomb squad that neutralized "suspicious objects" with water-filled condoms or the latest example of our Old English sheepdog's atrocious hygiene. But it took a while before I understood why the first of Safire's Ten Commandments for new columnists was "Skip the first six months."

When I replaced Tom Green, I was basically a reporter who had taken a two-year sabbatical on the editorial page. Now, I was a columnist with a long list of sources. I began calling them, interviewing them and quoting them. *Ad nauseum.* I filled my precious space with wallpaper-length quotations from people who were not me, and as I poured their words into the next day's column, my anxiety melted away. It was so easy to fill that space and I allowed myself to believe this job wasn't that tough after all.

Norman Cherniss's memo had laid out clear ground rules:

> *It is to be his column, which means he is to have*
> *maximum possible freedom. . . . Not the editor's*
> *[column] and not the [copy] desk's.*

If he had added, *"Not his wife's,"* I'm certain Cherniss would have made good on his pledge to find something else for me to do.

Sugar-coating was not my wife's style, particularly when it involved her unofficial job: the first and only civilian to read my column *before* it went to press. Candia's distaste for my chronic reliance on boring, space-consuming quotations revealed that she understood much more about column writing that I did. "Readers don't care what *they* think. They want to know what *you* think, whether they agree with you or not. That's why people read columns." I couldn't fire her. She was right. I had to replace the comforting fat with a meaty point of view. My point of view.

My column lived inside of me like a sophisticated kitchen appliance. Everything I heard, saw, read and did was automatically fed through a will-it-make-a-column strainer. The surviving residue became as vital to me as blood and oxygen. The strainer conditioned me to be selective and selfish. If something didn't rate Columnist's Gold, I had no use for it.

I learned that deadlines were lifelines. They forced me to write, rewrite, tweak and orchestrate words, phrases and crisp quotations into a tempo and rhythm that would hold readers' attention.

I learned that I would never bat 1.000, maybe not even .500. I clipped and framed a "Shoe" cartoon strip by Jeff MacNelly, with this caption: *"A column doesn't have to be spectacular every day. Just memorable. . . . Memorable enough to make your reader forget the garbage you wrote yesterday."*

I learned that "should" was a lethal enemy. The word reeked of obligation to fulfill someone else's expectations, not my own gut feeling. "Should" meant my heart wasn't in what I'd written. Worse, readers could tell. Readers always can tell.

"Want" helped me specialize in being a generalist. I wanted to write about what stirred, angered or amused me: a school district whose misguided unit on "critical thinking" asked students to decide whether the Holocaust actually happened; a postcard price war in Palm Springs and the staggering price of Dodger Dogs in Los Angeles; an arrogant "tough-on-crime" DA who once put a guy on trial for stealing three pieces of cactus valued at $1 (aghast at such a waste of their time and public money, the jury found him not guilty); a college neighborhood where rich Orange County investors bought houses and converted living rooms into multiple bedrooms, creating an Animal House subdivision teeming with students, automobiles, amplifiers, vomit and urine. While I drastically cut back on that wallpaper of quotations, I didn't hesitate to print the priceless nuggets that thoughtful readers often sent me. One day, the mail brought a photocopy of a sign posted in a government office that was undergoing renovation. "Sorry for the Incontinence."

I doled out nicknames: "Trafficula" for the new, gridlocked city of Temecula; "Cuddles" for that abrasive DA. I stole ideas. *San Francisco Chronicle* columnist Herb Caen wrote a year-ender that recognized people he had mentioned during the previous twelve months. My year-ender consisted solely of a list of people, except criminals, who had appeared in my column and deserved a thank-you for making my job easier. I avoided alphabetical order to keep readers engaged.

Once I'd sweated over it, written it, rewritten and hit "SEND," I began to forget what I had written. I had to find a new idea, make the calls and hope it didn't crumble under the weight of facts. Decide how to tell it to the readers. Beat another deadline. Ellen Goodman, a longtime columnist for the *Boston Globe*, recalled that someone once said, "writing a column is like being married to a nymphomaniac. Every time you think you're through, you have to do it again."

Dan Bernstein, columnist. COURTESY SOUTHERN CALIFORNIA NEWS GROUP.

"YOU DON'T ALWAYS have to be funny," Cherniss once told me. Some columns told heartbreaking stories: an in-custody mother who attended the funeral of the daughter she was accused of murdering; another mother who crawled into her dying daughter's hospital bed and later found the courage to speak to students about this beautiful young woman who overdosed at a party, among friends.

Other subjects allowed me to consider other options on the how-to-write menu. When I came across something that boiled my blood, my first impulse was to strike back with the fury and rectitude of a sledge-hammer-wielding preacher. But pontificating was not my long suit, so I forced myself to let time pass while I searched for a way to make the same point with a lighter touch. I called it humor or satire, although some found different ways to describe it.

"Here's the *sarcastic* one!" announced the British-accented employee when I entered the "Press Club" – the Jack-in-the-Box next to the paper. Others called me snarky. Still others seemed to appreciate how effectively a swatch of humor could cloak a dagger. "They never felt the knife slide in."

"You're the funniest columnist in America!" declared the caller, notifying me I had won a national contest. The recognition was immensely gratifying. But deciding what's funny is not a hard science. As I walked to the paper from the parking lot one spring morning, I was convinced that readers would think my just-published column was a flop. *I* thought it was funny. My wife was more reserved. "I hope they read the whole thing."

When I stepped into the newsroom, I felt the cold gaze of the normally genial woman who fielded readers' phone calls. She informed me that the editor wished to see me about my latest column. The editor's right-hand man had read it at his breakfast table and fumed, "Why didn't we have this on Page One?"

The lead item reported there had been a misprint on the federal 1040 form. A line that said "add" should have said "subtract." New forms would be issued. People who had filed early would have to refile. The column, which included several more fabricated items, concluded with my best wishes for a happy April Fool's Day.

When I entered the editor's lair, I learned that tax preparers, seniors who had already filed their returns and even a representative of the IRS had contacted the paper. My editor informed me that it wasn't my job to "jerk people's chains" and ordered me to write a correction, really an apology. Over the years, the story about this column has proven to be much funnier than the column itself.

At times, I decided music was the best way to convey a message. When John Sununu, the first President Bush's chief of staff, got caught flying to Aspen and Vail on U.S. military aircraft, sometimes with his wife in tow, I wrote a parody called Chattanooga Sununu. To my delight, the *Washington Post* printed it. National Public Radio found a female vocal group to sing it. I pictured George and Barbara Bush belting it out in the Oval Office:

Pardon me, George,
But are ya gonna sack Sununu?
We trust that you care
That we've been paying his fare.

We will assume
That things were fine as far as you knew;
The man's got his rights
But he should spring for his flights.

He left from DC with his Nancy
On a C-1-3-Oh.
Jetted off to Aspen
Where the forecast said snow.

Did a little skiing,
Maybe some sight-seeing,
Didn't bring his wallet.
What a human being!

Can you afford
To carry baggage like Sununu?
Satin and lace
More like a pop in the face.

At least make him pay
Whenever he may roam.
Oh, pay up, John Sununu,
Or kindly stay the hell home.

I NEVER ENVISIONED I'd dwell in the land of journalism for four-plus decades, a span when readers relied on newspapers, mostly trusted them and believed their paper was looking out for them. In 2014, I said good-bye to the *Press-Enterprise* readers who stuck with me and, along with my colleagues, fed me ideas that survived the strainer. I never set out to be a columnist, but with the help of these treasured enablers it turned out to be the perfect job for thirty-two years.

There Is Nothin' Like a Dame

ONCE I STARTED The Day Job, I didn't quit trombone cold turkey. Candia recalled that I played in a Salem jazz band – not because she ever attended a concert, but because she remembered the title of a thoroughly absorbing composition: "Advance of the Sponges." And there was that night in October 1975 when I sat in a Salem orchestra rehearsal, most likely counting rests, as Carlton Fisk slugged the walk-off homer in that classic Game 6 of the Boston Red Sox-Cincinnati Reds World Series. But when we moved to Riverside a year later, playing trombone slid down my priority list, giving way to a crash course in music appreciation. And whistling.

During these early Riverside years, I met Gregg Sieja as we watched our wives guide our dogs (or vice versa) through obedience training. Gregg had moved to Riverside from Detroit. Some of his musician friends had taken the same route, hoping to plant their flag on the SoCal music scene. Gregg played bass guitar with a deceptively vacant gaze. He was totally locked in on keeping perfect time. With me, he was totally focused on finding a cure for my ignorance.

"Are you hip to this?" he'd ask, plucking a record from the wall-to-wall shelves of vinyl in his small music room. He had hundreds of albums. Maybe thousands. Then, he'd introduce me to the air-tight wizardry of Frank Zappa; the Coasters' funny, forlorn "Shoppin' for Clothes" (*"That's a suit you'll never own"*); "Ring-a-Ding-Ding" and other albums by Frank Albert Sinatra; "Midnight in Moscow" and "Puttin' on the Ritz" by Kenny Ball and his Jazzmen; the Gatling-gun lyrics of Lambert Hendrix & Ross; John Coltrane's "Favorite Things"; Oscar Peterson's turbo-charged ticklers; Ella Fitzgerald and Miles Davis, who played with his back to us when we saw him at the Hollywood Bowl.

Before I met Gregg, I had dismissed Mel Tormé as a cloying, rubber-faced, chestnuts-roasting-on-an-open-fire dullard. "Listen to this!" Gregg commanded as the turntable arm landed on track after Tormé track. Now, I heard an elegant, energetic singer. His masterful blend of precision and imagination left me in awe, especially when he scatted along musical terrain I never knew existed.

Greg Sieja with the Three Stooges. Artist's collection.

Years later, after I met and interviewed Tormé and wrote a column that is reprinted in this book, I sent Gregg a photo of Mel and me standing side by side in our tuxes. It annoyed him no end. Gregg should have been in that photo. But at least it provided my mentor with tangible evidence that he had gotten through to me.

In 1977, to her eternal regret, Candia spotted a sprawling, two-page ad in *The New Yorker* magazine beckoning one and all to "The World's First International Whistle-Off." Yes, a whistling contest. May the best lips win.

I had been whistling since I was a kid. Whistling any tune that popped into my head as I walked through my Denver neighborhood: "Red Red Robbin," "Sweet Georgia Brown," "Rhapsody in Blue." I whistled "Peter and the Wolf" as I walked through a Palo Alto neighborhood, my signal to Candia that I was almost home. Almost always, I whistled alone.

But here I was in picturesque Carson City, Nevada, discovering a new culture, or cult: people who produced music without instruments. A buttoned-down barrister and a medical doctor, both Canadian, whistled classical music. A lawyer from Hawaii carried a tune by contorting his lips into a rubbery, oblong cavern. A New York cabbie whistled right through his cupped hands, producing a sound much like a recorder. A middle-aged woman from Orange County had been whistling since enrolling in Southern California's Agnes Woodward School of Whistling at age nine. An elderly Bay Area gentleman began to whistle only after cramming up to twenty cigars into his mouth. A rugged Calgary brakeman rode his pristine pucker to a championship or two, even as his pursuit of perfection made him a nervous wreck. We even had our own *prima donna*: a guy who refused to exit his trailer and make a grand entrance to the outdoor stage until there was total, absolute silence.

As soon as I saw that magazine ad, I phoned Mitch Hider, who had been a reporter at the *Capital Journal* in Oregon. Mitch whistled with the pluck and pizzazz of a Vaudevillian and eventually won a championship and became the emcee at annual competitions in the U.S. and Japan. In Carson City, we became a duet, at one point whistling "Let Me Call You Sweetheart" to our moms, who joined us on stage dressed as Whistler's Mothers. Though they were good sports, they had to be shaking their heads. *For this, we sent them to college?*

Dan Bernstein (center) and Mitch Hider serenade Oregon Governor Vic Atiyeh at the 1979 Oregon State Fair, where Hider was the "Fair Whistler," hired to entertain visitors. Here, they whistle "Alabama Bound." UPI PHOTO.

Over the years, I won a trophy or two in a relatively minor category, novelty whistling, once by belting out "Autumn Leaves" while accompanying myself with a leaf blower. But it was a colossal flop that taught me a lesson about performing – and writing. This time, I was backing myself with an electric typewriter as I whistled "I'm Gonna Sit Right Down and Write Myself A Letter." Though I thought my act was going quite well, others thought it was going quite long. When I stepped off the stage, a tall, elderly gentleman known in showbiz as Dr. Horatio Q. Birdbath intercepted me. Doc Birdbath had performed with Spike Jones and His City Slickers, a 1940s–50s band that specialized in tightly composed musical spoofs. He could mimic the sounds of birds, which made him eminently qualified to judge whistlers. At that moment, however, he counseled me as an old pro who had seen the very best – and the very worst. "Son," he said, draping his long arm over my shoulder, "Always leave 'em wanting more."

1981 Whistle-off, Carson City; Category: Whistling with Novel Accompaniment. *Dan whistles and sings "Medflies" to the tune of "Blue Skies," while wearing banana ears and a suit to look like Governor Jerry Brown; Mitch, dressed as a fly, is the novel accompaniment. Won 1st prize!*

WHILE ATTENDING WHISTLING contests and the Gregg Sieja Conservatory of Music put my trombone on the back burner (only figuratively speaking), the burner was simmering. Simon Sykes, a *Press-Enterprise* reporter-editor, who also played trombone, introduced me to Riverside's small but pulsating Dixieland jazz scene. I became an irregular at Sunday jam sessions held at an old Moose Lodge. These were afternoons of eating, drinking and, for newcomers like me, ever so briefly playing. We'd sign in, pull up a chair and wait to be summoned for a quick set of three or four tunes. I'd never heard of some and didn't know which key to play others. (Think of "key" as a uniform. If every bagpiper wore plaid kilts except for the one in red-striped clown pants, that piper is off key.)

But these small Dixieland groups – usually a trumpet, clarinet, trombone, drums and bass and maybe a banjo – were stacked with veterans who did what they could to protect newcomers from humiliation. It also helped that Dixieland is rigidly flexible: Once a melody is established, the tune becomes a kaleidoscope of improvisation. Proficient players sail effortlessly through various key changes, unveiling new ideas or showing off their road-tested licks.

This didn't describe me when my Moose Lodge Sundays found me on the hot seat. But they helped me realize I had inherited my mother's ear, allowing me to pick out the proper notes and correctly guess the next key that lurked just around the corner. Sometimes, I simply crashed and burned. Fortunately, these jam sessions usually sold beer.

The backdrop to all of this – the whistling, Gregg's music tutorials and the Moose Lodge rambles – was that demanding Day Job. True, I wallowed in the freedom that defined it, but I also had to come up with idea after idea to produce column after column. So I didn't hesitate to break out my trombone, oil my slide and squeeze into a uniform on the balmy autumn night I joined the La Sierra High School Screaming Eagles' Marching Band for my first halftime show since 1971 in Pasadena.

My band mates had humored me during the week of field practices and I managed to play decently enough under the Friday night lights. But returning to my bleacher seat, I wasn't sure I'd gathered quite enough material to uphold the solemn code of my line of work: "He'll do *anything* for a column." As I fretted, I overheard a young spectator say, "Do you see that old man in the band uniform?" Old? I was still safely in my 30s. The little punk stung me, but only until I realized that his well-placed zinger was pure gold. Just like that, I knew I had enough to write a column.

I didn't write about my musical escapades that often. There weren't that many of them. But they sometimes led to a gig. Long after that halftime show, Riverside's Ramona High School invited me to play in a couple of musicals, *Damn Yankees* and *South Pacific*. The latter landed me in the pit right next to Mr. Robinson – a kind, friendly "Robby," not a stuffy "Robert." If I seemed old to that teenaged wise guy in the bleachers, Robby seemed old to me, even though by then I was a middle-aged newspaperman who was rapidly losing his hair. Robby played lead trombone and I knew right away that all I had to do was listen to him, follow him, watch the conductor and try not to watch the show. Robby played with ease and confidence. The music may have been simple for him, but he respected it and played it the way the composer and conductor wanted it to be played. And he seemed to really enjoy those nights in the pit, something I found inspiring and calming.

When we weren't playing, I learned a few things about Robby. He was in his seventies – just as I am now. He lived in Orange County and had pretty much been playing trombone all his life. But that's about all I could get out of him. Much as he loved to play his trombone, Robby refused to toot his own horn.

Not long after the *South Pacific* run concluded, Robby began sending me photocopies of trombone solos I'm sure he had mastered: "Bolero," "Darn that Dream" complete with reproduced coffee stains and penciled-in notes, "Sophisticated Lady," Hoagy Carmichael's "Stardust," and the standard for which Tommy Dorsey set the standard: "I'm Gettin' Sentimental Over You." I still have those solos. I treasure them, practice them and have yet to master them.

Ours was a short-lived correspondence, but I later ran across a newspaper article that revealed a lot more about Robby Robinson. He was 84 when *Orange County Register* reporter Timothy Mangan wrote a profile describing Robby as the "gentle, friendly guy" with the "sunny attitude," a "jolly" trombonist who had played in big bands and jazz combos since the 1930s. He had backed a few artists whose names never came up during our chats: Judy Garland, Nat King Cole, Tony Bennett and Sinatra. He played in bands led by Harry James, Tommy Dorsey and Spike Jones, who once chased him around the stage and squirted him with water after he missed a note. Robby spent fourteen hours in a studio one day in the 1950s when a beautiful actress proved to be so fatally self-conscious and shy that she couldn't record a song in the presence of other people. After she left, the orchestra recorded the song without her. The next day Marilyn Monroe returned to the studio and, alone at last, had no trouble laying down her vocal track – a tune from *Some Like It Hot*.

During World War II, Robby Robinson joined the Army Air Corps, where he was plucked out of mess duty and plopped into a band. Something similar had happened to my old trombone teacher, Tasso Harris, who got recruited for a band in the Navy. It made me wonder if they'd ever met. It's possible. Robby and Tasso are listed as personnel in *The Complete Capitol Recordings of Gene Krupa & Harry James*.

I've thought about Tasso many times over the years, particularly during the Day Job hours when that word – *initiative* – jolted me into making a tough phone call or *not* waiting for a return call or rewriting the next day's column yet again in hopes that readers wouldn't have to slog through it. I also wondered what Tasso would have thought about this former student. Perhaps satisfaction or surprise that my random forays into the local music scene showed I still had a passion for trombone. I might have just continued this on-and-off dabbling if a dinner party hadn't set me on a path and would periodically leave my wife lamenting, "I'm playing second fiddle to a third trombone."

CHAPTER 8

All That Jazz

"YOU WERE PLAYING with your eyes closed," grinned Roger Rickson, not breaking stride as he walked off the stage.

It was after a 1980s concert featuring the Riverside City College Evening Jazz Ensemble. I played a solo that night – a rarity for me – and, yes, my eyes were shuttered. Not because I had committed anything to memory, but because I had never learned to read the hieroglyphics that most musicians recognize as chord changes. I played by ear in plain view of a guy who never missed a beat – or an eye that didn't blink.

Rickson was the soul of the community college's jazz program. Also, the concrete and rebar. Talking about RCC jazz without recognizing Roger Rickson's immense influence is a misdemeanor in parts of Riverside County.

He arrived at RCC in the 1970s and built the jazz program the way a coach builds a dynasty. He cared deeply about his students, even those who would likely stash their horns when they heard the clarion calls of Adulthood, Family and Responsibility. He created opportunities for them, motivated them and messed with them. He once told a high school trumpet player who had a gift for playing flat to go home and saw off part of his tuning slide. To Rickson's chagrin, the kid did just that.

Like any successful coach, Rickson knew recruitment was crucial. In the jazz world that meant staging festivals that showcased the college while providing high-school jazz bands with critiques and master classes by professional musicians. He had hosted those kinds of fests as a high school band director in nearby in Corona. Soon, he was hosting them at RCC. One attracted a Riverside high-school prospect named Charlie Richard, who eventually enrolled at the college. Years later, Charlie told the local newspaper that Rickson was "the single most important and encouraging person for me in my career."

Charlie and I arrived in Riverside in 1976. I was in my mid-twenties, a new business reporter struggling to compute simple percentages for unemployment stories. Charlie was a teenaged Arkansas-born traveler, an Air Force brat who had been deployed to Riverside's Ramona High School when his dad landed at March Air Force Base. By that time, the family had toured the world, including Mississippi – twice. It was during that second Mississippi swing that fifth-grader Charlie visited "a bit of a petting zoo" where future band members got their first look at domesticated musical instruments. Drawn to a shiny object resting in a case, Charlie decided he wanted to play saxophone. He eventually learned to play all the saxophones – soprano, alto, tenor and baritone. Clarinet and flute, too.

I met Charlie when I joined the Riverside City College night jazz band after a guy at a dinner party urged me to check it out. Charlie had transferred to Cal State LA, where he would earn his master's degree. But his ties to RCC were unbreakable. He loved the place and loved playing in the night band. In the early 1990s, not long after we met, Charlie joined RCC Music Department faculty. He soon became director of a group of adults that included a balding trombone player who had once been spotted playing with his eyes closed.

THE RCC EVENING JAZZ ENSEMBLE, as it has been known for years, is a big band, population roughly eighteen, with a demographic that includes saxes, trumpets, trombones and a rhythm section. Most members hold down day jobs, many are school band directors or music profs and even direct their own jazz bands and arrange and compose music. I've played in the Monday group off and on for decades. Sometimes, the day job or other musical adventures pulled me away. But I have always been welcomed back, which has made me feel grateful and, on occasion, terrified.

The music, much of it composed or arranged by band members, is artfully crafted and occasionally (for me) treacherous. This band is loaded with nimble musicians who play at a high level, even if they're looking at a tune for the first time. I'm not quite in that league, especially with up-tempo pieces where notes whiz by like a bullet train as my trombone slide (and brain) marinate in molasses. Numerous times, I've recalled the words of that deadpan comic, George Gobel, who once told Johnny Carson: "The whole world is a tuxedo and I'm a pair of brown shoes." There is only one promising antidote to these brown-shoe moments. Practice.

I took my music home and set my metronome (no vintage time piece, just a free digital app) to what Charlie calls *tempo de learno*. This allowed me to digest daunting passages as if I were dining on a plus-size elephant: one delectable measure at a time. Though I had to practice to keep up, learn the music and reduce unforced errors, there was much more to it than self-defense. Practicing, like going to the gym, is absolutely essential to staying in shape. If my health club had been stocked with an array of lip weights and a sanitary mouth-muscle machine, I might have become a regular.

Charlie Richard, director of the Riverside City College Evening Jazz Ensemble.
Courtesy Riverside City College.

I was not an obsessive practitioner. Not like my sister, Paula, the talented teenage violist who logged countless hours in front of the bathroom mirror. But I tried to get in at least ninety minutes at least four times a week. I truly missed it when I failed to keep to the schedule. On practice days, I shut myself up in a small room far enough away from my wife and dogs to defend myself against charges of disturbing the peace. Sometimes, I had a plan: practice music I had to learn for a concert. Sometimes, I just winged it, running through music I loved to play or hadn't played in ages. Sometimes, I played the solos Robby Robinson sent me or picked out a jazz tune from a play-along book and, backed by the recorded rhythm section, listened to the chord changes and practiced improvising.

Along the way, I learned things that hadn't been obvious to me at all. When I inhaled, I was accustomed to socking away a fresh supply of oxygen in my chest, which, as far as storage compartments go, was convenient and effective. But I discovered that when playing trombone, the proper storage compartment was located about a foot south. Storing the air below the beltway and propelling it upwards produced a richer sound and increased my endurance. It also took some pressure off of my deeply imprinted trombone mouth, which had been carrying far more than its fair share of the load.

I also discovered that practicing actually worked. I could feel and hear the results. And it provided an unexpected fringe benefit: practicing whisked me away from the day job, the deadlines, the chronic angst of not knowing what I was going to write about next, the creeping cringes when I thought about the stinker of a column that had been delivered to tens of thousands of homes that very day. Practicing commanded my full attention, allowing me to slip into a state of mind where nothing else mattered and time just melted away. It also yielded a dividend that was even greater than any personal accomplishment: the satisfaction of playing in an ensemble where all the moving parts ultimately meshed as precisely and musically as the composer and band leader intended.

Playing with a group of musicians was such a stark contrast from my day job. Not that a columnist is journalism's version of a solo act. My colleagues dug up stories and provided me with fodder. Readers fed me countless ideas. Editors saved me from myself. And Candia came up with her own ideas and vetoed my lousy ones. Even so, I often felt marooned on an island, luxuriating in the freedom (sometimes laced with panic) to decide what to write about and how to write it. Which was pretty much the polar opposite of an ensemble.

RCC Evening Jazz Ensemble, performing at Mario's Place in downtown Riverside. 'Bone section (left to right): Bill Saulnier, Danny Balancio, Jennifer Hall, Dan Bernstein. Courtesy Riverside City College.

The RCC night jazz band has taught me to listen to things besides the sounds I produce and manufacture in my capacity as third trombone. I listen to the person sitting immediately to my right because he or she is usually the first, or lead, trombone. How loudly or softly is the lead playing? How does the lead play a note, shape a phrase? The lead calls the shots. The second trombone is often the designated soloist. The bass trombone is kind of a hybrid – the anchor of the trombone section but also an anchor of the whole band, often in cahoots with the bass and the baritone sax.

The third trombone is tucked into the section of the band that literally sets the tone: We lay down the foundation, introducing the harmony and playing the chords that define a particular piece. The saxes and trumpets extend these chords, often taking them to stratospheric, contortionist levels. But without the foundation? Picture a glittering Manhattan skyscraper topped by a posh penthouse occupied exclusively by saxes and trumpets. If the building's foundation ever gave way, the penthouse would likely collapse, strewing those trumpets and saxophones in a heap of wreckage. Trombone players resist every opportunity to point this out. We simply hoist the penthouse on our shoulders and play on.

In addition to listening to one another, all sections are duty-bound to listen to the lead trumpet player, who, along with other trumpets, is conveniently located directly behind the trombone section. This makes it impossible *not* to listen. But it's not just about volume. We listen to how the lead attacks or releases or hardly plays a note. We listen to the rhythm section because the drummer and bass player are the band's heartbeat which can accelerate to a Psycho-shower-scene frenzy, only to lapse into a Malibu-yoga-studio trance. All in the same piece.

The most discerning listener of all is the quiet man who sits in front of this wall of sound. A man who, at a young age received national recognition as a jazz composer. A musician who has performed with the Los Angeles Philharmonic, Pasadena Symphony, The Nelson Riddle Orchestra, The Four Tops and his mom's favorite group, The Temptations. A band director whose top RCC student jazz ensemble has become a dynasty, winning national competitions sponsored by *DownBeat* magazine year after year after year. Charlie Richard, this quiet man, has big-time chops.

It is not lost on him that most of the musicians in the night band are capable of much more than playing what they see on the page. They can imagine and execute subtle, deft touches that make those notes fly or float off the page. But first, Charlie must be satisfied that the ensemble has accomplished the basics: good pitch, good time, good balance. He is uncannily attuned to the note held too long or not long enough, the breath that shouldn't have been taken, the beat that lagged or inexplicably bolted from the chute, the lone instrument or entire section that brayed so coarsely or meowed so meekly that the delicate balance that defines an ensemble was mortally wounded. "If you get the balance wrong or the sound is too loud, it's not musical."

And if it's not musical? Charlie once called our attention to *Whiplash*, a 2014 film about a promising young drummer and the perfectionist band director whose solution to "not musical" stopped just short of homicide. It was a movie about a jazz band, but it certainly wasn't about Charlie Richard, who has the clean-cut appearance and wardrobe of a Land's End lifer. No matter what might be swirling around him, Charlie manages to keep his voice at please-pass-the-salt room temperature even though he admits, "It's not my natural inclination since my dad was a chief master sergeant." The most hostile word I've ever heard Charlie utter in a rehearsal is, *"Rats!"*

Jennifer Hall played lead trombone for Charlie when she was a student in the late 1990s. She retains vivid memories of what happens when something is not musical:

> He doesn't have to say anything. He kind of purses his
> lips and gives you that look like he's so disappointed
> in you. You never want to see it again. It always made
> you want to impress him more.

I'M COMFORTABLE in the third-trombone chair, privileged and downright lucky to occupy it in this band. But whenever I page through a new piece of music, I hope – and dread – that it will call for a solo. This hardly ever happens. But once, when such a part landed on my music stand, the timing could not have been better.

A few months earlier, there had been a trombone solo for the taking. The better players in the section put it up for grabs. Who wants it? I did. But I didn't have the nerve or audacity to speak up. Driving home from rehearsal that night, I let myself have it. *What did you have to lose? You're an old man! What are you waiting for?*

Now, I had another chance. The part in front of me had a solo. Hope had been fulfilled. But the dread thrummed like the soundtrack to *Jaws.* The chord changes staring back at me might as well have been written in Mandarin. I had my work cut out for me. I had a week to practice, and the fear of being embarrassed turned out to be well-founded.

At the next rehearsal, when the time arrived for The Great Unveiling, I roared out of the gate like a greyhound on steroids. I reached the transition from funk to reggae at least a lap ahead of the pack, all the while littering the track with a trail of notes that were not meant to be played – or heard.

The band played on as if nothing had happened while I played on knowing nothing good had happened. Charlie didn't say a word. I couldn't bring myself to look at him, fearing I'd see what Jennifer Hall described as the telltale signs of disappointment: those pursed lips and that certain look. I was so mortified that I swallowed my pride (by then the size of a pellet of puppy chow) and asked for help. A couple of bandmates gave me pretty much the same advice: Just listen. Don't worry about the notes. Don't try to do too much. Just listen to the rhythm section and stay in the groove.

For the next week, I played along with an audio track, at first just concentrating on listening to the drums and the bass. Once I locked in on the time, it became easier to find the notes, to tailor a solo to the sounds and rhythms I heard and felt, to improvise without memorizing, which could have been fatal. If I drew a blank, I liked my chances of going full-on catatonic. On the night of the concert, I took my pre-arranged deep breath (this really helped), listened to the band and kept it simple. After weeks of angst and still more in-car lecturing – *Stop worrying! This is supposed to be fun! There are people out there with REAL problems!* – I felt surprisingly relaxed as I stayed in the groove for the duration of my solo: all forty seconds of it.

THE PANDEMIC CHALLENGED the conventional definition of everything from "rehearsal" to "musical." Imagine a jazz band that doesn't meet on a stage or in a band room, but in a room called Zoom, where each player, instrument in hand, is incarcerated in a small square. For that matter, imagine a community jazz band even meeting during a pandemic as beleaguered RCC profs scrambled for ways to teach, motivate and care for suddenly isolated students. During breaks in these gloom-and-Zoom rehearsals, band members who taught high school traded stories about young musicians defecting in droves, perhaps never to return. (Even the geekiest of band geeks found it hard to pretend a Zoom marching band was a marching band.) But Charlie and Kevin Mayse, the lead trumpet and also an RCC professor, decided to keep the Monday night jazz ensemble going.

For almost the entire Fall 2020 semester, we "met" each week, played our instruments but never heard each other play a single note. We muted ourselves and played along to sound tracks. Only one person could hear the result: Charlie. The second semester, we switched to a software that allowed us to listen to each other and even tweak individual volumes, making it easier to hear the drums, bass, section leaders and any soloist. It was truly slick – except for the times we started a tune at the same instant, counted ever so carefully and still sounded like a five o'clock pile-up on a SoCal freeway. Speeds varied as our individual sounds traveled through cyberspace. Individual volumes did, too. Mine was so red-zone hot that, even after adjusting certain "settings," I had to turn my back on my laptop – and my bandmates – and point my horn in the general direction of Neptune.

On May 24, 2021, the RCC Evening Jazz Ensemble had its final rehearsal of the school year. For the first time in nine months, we were software-free. We met in person, in a downtown parking structure. For one glorious night only, the jazz ensemble became a garage band. It felt like a high school reunion without the nametags and cosmetic surgery. It just felt good to be sitting side-by-side (at a CDC-sanctioned distance) again. To see each other, hear each other, talk to each other, kid each other and record several tunes together, hoping Charlie would deem them sufficiently musical to share with an online audience.

Even though we played in a parking garage and attracted an audience of fewer than a dozen, our Monday night concert stirred memories of the "normal" past when we performed at area high schools, hoping to attract new generations of musicians to what Charlie called "a little community college in Riverside."

We also performed at events that proved rich in unintended comic relief: At a dinner-fundraiser for the local symphony, the program ran so long that when we finally started to play the dance floor was far less populated than the aisles leading to the exits. We played on, briefly, until the auditorium clean-up crew began flapping tablecloths and breaking down tables: our cue to wrap it up before they revved up the in-house choir of vacuum cleaners.

Most memorable, though, are the concerts on our home court, a "school for the arts" that opened in downtown Riverside in 2015. It's really not a school for the arts at all, but every inch a *music* school, with a performance hall that might well have achieved acoustical perfection.

All designed with the advice and consent of the music faculty and with meticulous attention to the school's most prized resource: students.

Our concerts in the Coil School for the Arts included those annual jazz festivals that drew bands from all over Southern California as well as a whoozwho of mainly SoCal jazz artists who conducted master classes and performed for the high schoolers. These concerts found the RCC Evening Jazz Ensemble bursting with peak energy. Our pitch was perfect, or nearly so, and the time and balance left Charlie's lips mostly unpursed. The soloists nestled in their zones of creativity and spontaneity and the audience of prospective RCC students whooped it up as only student whoopers can whoop.

After three decades at RCC, Charlie marveled, "There is no way we had any idea things would be this good." And there was no way I could have imagined that, decades after a dinner party where I heard about a night jazz band at a community college, I'd be sitting in the trombone section as my personal odometer cruised past seventy. Quite an eye-opener, especially for someone who plays with his eyes closed.

CHAPTER 9

I Love a Noisy Trombone

I REJOINED THE RCC Evening Jazz Ensemble in 2014 after a long stretch with a brass quintet and an even longer stretch with the *Press-Enterprise*. I retired after thirty-six years.

I did not return to a band room of strangers. Charlie and Kevin gave me a heartwarming welcome home. I was delighted to see that Kris Parish, a high school band director and a marvelous trumpet soloist, was still there. No online matchmaker would have paired a conservative Christian with a liberal Jew who didn't read chord changes. But we had become friends. One night, standing outside the building where we rehearsed, I pointed to Riverside's new downtown library and told Kris its large, whale-shaped window struck me as a clever literary reference to *Moby Dick*. Kris gazed at it for a moment and replied, "Jonah."

I was more than relieved to see John Sandhagen. In addition to being a key anchor to the band, this unflappable – and usually sockless – bass trombonist was my unofficial time keeper. Whenever I got lost, I'd glance down at his hands, where thick fingers toted up the exact number of measures that had elapsed during a prolonged rest period.

If I wore a watch, I could set it to Bill Dickson's bass and never lose a second. Bill earned a special place in my heart when he told me his dad always read my column. Jeff Benedict, a fellow Denver boy, was a masterful sax player and composer with a sharp eye for cultural dinosaurs. When we played his "Fotomat Song (Someday My Prints Will Come)," I became so nostalgic that I felt like I was sixty-five again.

And Sandy Megas was not only a fine pianist and brilliant composer, but a reliable gust of fresh, sardonic wit.

But returning to the trombone section was almost like moving into a new neighborhood. Though Sandhagen had a lock on bass bone, the first and second seats were occupied by people I'd never met and soon would come to admire and appreciate. Both of them made me a better player. Jennifer Hall and Danny Balancio (his mom prefers Daniel) had much in common. Both were native Californians, born in the '70s and supremely talented. At one time or another, each played lead and I sat next to them. A ringside seat at a very low price. Though they had seriously considered careers as performing musicians, both had day jobs, kids and faced the challenge that has dogged countless others: How to do their jobs, care for their families and still satisfy the craving to keep playing the instrument they loved. It wasn't always easy. At times, it proved nearly impossible.

Danny Balancio

When I met Danny, he sported spiky hair, Clark Kent glasses and a toothpaste smile. He played trombone like a monster who performed brain surgery: a powerful, roaring sound that could be quieted to a whisper and delivered with the delicacy of a doily.

Danny Balancio, trombone. Courtesy Danny Balancio.

Thirty years earlier, he was a kid who knew nothing about jazz. He just knew he was in love with his sixth-grade teacher. One day, he sat right next to Miss Kotish among a sea of other sixth graders who had been invited to hear a top-notch high school jazz band in Eagle Rock, near Pasadena. It was a basically recruitment concert staged by a nationally known director who at one point picked up his trumpet and soloed with his band. Danny noticed that Miss Kotish was so moved that she began to cry. "I said, 'Man! I want that power!' That was the start. Right then."

Danny's career as an Eagle Rock drummer lasted two weeks before the director, desperate to plug holes in his ensemble, asked, "Why don't you play the trombone? It's easy." He tried it and loved it. Inspired by "an amazing caliber of jazz musicians" he got to school for the seven-thirty jam sessions and went back to the band room during lunch. They practiced scales and improvised in a new key every day. Danny thought this was normal. "If you just put this stuff in front of kids and say this is what you've got to learn, you just do it. You have no frame of reference. Later on, you get out and get exposure to other things and realize, 'Shit! It was really hard!'" After graduating in 1993, Danny went to Pasadena City College, joined the jazz band and made a shocking discovery. "We were playing charts that I played in ninth grade."

Armed with music scholarships, he became a music major, but a jealous rival wouldn't leave him alone. Technology, computers, games! He couldn't get enough of it. The 1990s saw Danny dancing the trombone/high-tech two step.

At PCC, fellow musicians told him they practiced four or five hours a day. Danny decided to practice six. Some nights, in deference to his dad, who didn't "want to hear that racket," Danny drove his 1985 Jeep to a parking lot, climbed into the back, behind the driver's seat, and "practiced diagonally," pointing his slide toward the front passenger seat. "This is where I grew most as a musician."

Tech was growing on him, too. He went to work for a "mom and pop" chain called Egghead Software and landed another at Earthlink when the financially troubled Egghead laid him off. Still playing his trombone, Danny immersed himself in the LA salsa scene and also became a member of the University of Southern California jazz band even though he never went to USC. The two-step was in high gear.

Music seemed to nose ahead of tech support when, in 1999, he was invited to go on the road with "this one-hit wonder named Lou Bega." Turned out the one-hit wonder was opening for a singer named Cher on her "Do You Believe" tour. Danny started to think, "All right. I could try to do music."

He toured big cities in the U.S. and Canada and during a three-day break, the warm-up act flew to Chile to perform in a festival. When Cher's tour ended, Danny quit Earthlink. For the next three weeks, he and the Bega band toured South America. "Now, *we* were the headliner." Danny was twenty-four and on a roll.

But the roll was slowing down. Though he received a trickle of residuals from TV-show performances, his music world was quiet. Crickets. There was no social media. Danny had to hustle for work. "People see you on TV and they don't realize you're at home trying to get your next gig. I stuck it out for a year. I really struggled." Then came a moment of clarity: USC offered him a scholarship. "That was the final decision for me. I said, 'No. I don't want to major in music.'" Danny had reached the fork in the road. He took the one paved with gold: high tech.

As the new century raced through its first decade, Danny got married, had kids and realized he could make good money by being both the real-world guy who understood what business people wanted to get done and the tech nerd who could explain to the geeks what those biz people needed to *get* it done. Things were clicking right along until the Great Recession stopped him cold.

The Riverside County Health Department, which had hired him in 2008, laid him off in 2009. His next job as an info-tech man lasted four months. His next job came with the fringe benefit of a long commute. But after seven years, he took a "big jump" to develop software that would manage a bunch of warehouses. When his boss disappeared, Danny got laid off again. Compared to high tech, a career in music looked like a civil service gig in the Department of Commerce.

During some of this time, Danny was still playing salsa gigs. He no longer worked the phone; the phone worked him. When it rang, there was a gig. He put it on the calendar. Salsa and unemployment checks got the family through some tough times. But eventually, nightclub work with nightclub hours caused tension. His wife "kind of drew a line." He stopped playing. "It was a very, very difficult time for me." It lasted two years.

When I met Danny, he had unpacked his trombone and come "home." He was back where he wanted to be: in a community college jazz band, often playing lead trombone in the RCC Evening Jazz Ensemble. "It was definitely a calling. That's where it all started for me."

In his book *Underground Railroad*, Colson Whitehead wrote:

> *There are instruments and human players but some-
> times a fiddle or a drum makes instruments of those
> who play them.*

He could have been describing Danny Balancio. Back in the Eagle Rock days, when his high school band entered jazz contests, the judges couldn't help noticing this trombone player. The taped comments would say things like, "Who's that kid bouncing over there? Straighten him up. Straighten him down." It was no use trying.

At first, I found it distracting, this lead trombone player juddering and lurching as if first chair was plugged in. But it was also contagious. He was the lead. He was pumped up and having fun, especially during concerts. Soon, I was lurching right along with him, feeding off the audience and the musicians around me. This is what Danny had missed during those dark years. "It's an immeasurable energy that I can tap into, it's an excitement that I thrive on." Back home in a jazz band, he became a cheerleader and a motivator, insistent that we match his sound to maintain balance. The Balancio Bounce was optional.

As a soloist, Danny was fearless, drawing on his salsa years as well as those fast times at Eagle Rock and Pasadena City College where improv became second nature. He'd be listening to the radio on the way to a concert, hear a slice of a solo and decide right then and there to find a way to work it into his solo. Or, as solo time approached, he'd listen to the drummer and the first notes out of his horn would mimic the rhythm the drummer had just played. He was spontaneous, unafraid to take chances, and, as happens to everyone in live concerts, things didn't always work out as planned. A bad note "can easily eat you up, really dig in on your confidence." But not for long. "Come on, man," Danny would tell himself. "You know what you're doing."

The Great Recession finally ended and so did the two-step. Danny hired on at UC Riverside with a full-time job and a mouthful of a title.

He left the night band, returned to salsa and got lucrative work in bands that played pop music at weddings and retirement parties. At this writing, he was back in the night band, playing lead trombone. Through it all, his memory of Danny the sixth-grader watching a concert in Eagle Rock (*"That was the start. Right then."*) has been preserved in amber. I like to think there are brief but heartfelt moments when he channels his inner Jimmy Durante and merrily growls, "Good night, Miss Kotish, wherever you are!"

Jennifer Hall

Jennifer was a natural. The word never even made a cameo in our conversations, but it was the background music to her story. She was born near San Francisco, the only child of high-school sweethearts who had no apparent musical interests at all, though her dad maintains he once wailed away on bongos.

Jennifer entered elementary school after the family moved to Chico. When the "music store guy" brought a carload of instruments to her class, she was smitten ... with the violin. "I wanted to play it so bad." By her own account, that's exactly what happened. She switched to trumpet. Not long afterwards, Jennifer's family inherited an upright piano. She used her trumpet to decode the notes on the piano keys and eventually discovered an oasis of calm: playing Bach and Mozart, even after the upright was banished to a musty garage when the family moved to Riverside County. When she entered middle school in Hemet, Jennifer had yet to touch a trombone.

She learned to play baritone (think pint-sized tuba) because her middle school teacher needed someone to play it. Next, she took up tuba because there arose a pressing need for a tuba player. As a sophomore, the arc of Jennifer's musical path once again was shaped by the irresistible force she called "We Need This." This time, her teacher needed a trombone player. There was no talk about trombone being a "boys' instrument." One of her teacher's best students ever had been another Jennifer: Jennifer Krupa went on to study at Julliard, perform with Wynton Marsalis and The Lincoln Center Jazz Orchestra, join the U.S. Navy's Commodores Jazz Ensemble and more. "He was so proud to have had her," said Jennifer Hall, "and always talked about her."

Now her teacher needed another trombone player and asked his latest Jennifer to "mess around with it and let him know." She messed around and let him know. "This was my instrument. I loved it."

Jennifer Hall, trombone. PHOTO BY DAN BERNSTEIN.

SHE PLAYED LEAD TROMBONE in West Valley High School's jazz band, the acknowledged "underdog" to the neighboring Hemet High jazz band, directed by Jeff Tower, a giant among jazz educators. But school boundaries could not tether Jennifer's talent. Tower invited her to play in his community college jazz band. She was repeatedly selected to play in Southern California's high-school honor jazz bands. She made it into a prestigious summer jazz program in the mountain community of Idyllwild. In her spare time, she played soccer, ran cross country, worked at a doctor's office and rang up a 4.0 GPA.

In 1995, Jennifer enrolled at Riverside City College, knowing the school's "music program was better than most." Her stay at RCC was brief – less than two academic years – but more than enough time to make an impression. She majored in music performance, playing as much as she could in concert band, trombone quartets, brass quintets and, of course, jazz band. She easily hurdled one of the toughest obstacles confronting any promising musician: seeing something cold and playing it hot.

> I love sight reading. I feel like it's from piano, which
> is hard because it's two hands. If you're only reading
> one line [of music], it's pretty easy.

It didn't take long for Charlie Richard to recognize the purity of Jennifer's talent. "She was remarkable – smart, industrious. Everything was so together. She was one of the best lead players I ever had and a great sight reader. I thought she was going to become a professional musician."

She became a mom instead. In December 1997, just days after playing her final recital ("I was huge – like *big!*"), she gave birth to Sean, a bouncing baby future trumpet player. The top-of-the-line trombone her parents bought her when she was in high school returned to its case for a lengthy hibernation.

By the time I met Jennifer, she had returned from the East Coast, where she cared for the baby during the day and worked nights when her husband, an Army enlistee, got off duty. Back in Hemet, she landed a job with the state gaming commission, inside an Indian casino. Next, she became a dispatcher for the Riverside County Sheriff's Department. Adept at simultaneously watching TV, crocheting and/or gaming on her phone, Jennifer was well-suited to field emergency calls, talk to deputies, call the fire department and run records on "subjects" to see if they had outstanding warrants. In 2018, partially through adroit social-media tracking, she and co-workers helped foil a planned attack on a college campus. As she steadily carved out her career, Jennifer added a daughter and subtracted a husband. The gold-plated Bach 16? Still snoozing in the case.

It is ironic, or maybe just fitting, that the trombone was finally awakened by the person who helped put it to bed. Jennifer's son, Sean, had taken up trumpet and was doing the same things his mom did: working very hard and playing very well. Now a teenager, he was accepted to that same summer jazz program Jennifer had attended. When she drove up the mountain to Idyllwild to see her son perform, Jennifer ran into a lot of people she knew, including that old teacher who thought she was one of the best lead players he'd ever had. Before long, Jennifer joined Charlie Richard and the RCC night jazz ensemble, a move that would have occurred even sooner if her friend and co-worker hadn't needed a kidney. Jennifer had one to spare. Once she recovered from the surgery, Jennifer was back at RCC just as Sean was making a name for himself in the school's top jazz band. Mother and son were performing in different jazz bands, sometimes on the same night, in the same concert hall. Their names were displayed on the same program.

JENNIFER'S SMILE COULD light up a subdivision, but it disappears when the mouthpiece touches her lips. When I sat beside her as she played lead trombone, I could feel her intensity. She reminded me of the hawk that resides at the peak of a giant eucalyptus near my backyard. It is entirely possible that Jennifer didn't view musical notes as prey, but she saw them and attacked them, no matter how fast or how high. Rhythmic zigs and zags didn't faze her. She played with authority. She also played with style, introducing unique brush strokes that the rest of the section could hear and follow.

> Jazz is much more expressive, more fun [than other
> music]. It's more you're playing because you know it
> as opposed to reading the music. I like how you can
> kind of stand out a little bit, but you still have the
> support of your section.

But playing alone in the spotlight made her feel unprotected.

> I don't enjoy soloing. I'm not really an outgoing
> person. I'm very quiet. I'm not even good about
> saying good morning.

Music allowed her to make "the connection with other people" without saying a word. "You're interacting with somebody, but it's not in the typical way. You're just playing together. That's always been my favorite: playing in an ensemble and ending up with a finished song."

When Jennifer told me her story, she was working the overnight shift in sheriff's dispatch and had left the jazz band because there was no way to squeeze in evening rehearsals and concerts. She was also raising Leanna, her teenaged daughter – "definitely my best friend...

a free spirit, creative, unapologetically confrontational. Pretty much everything the opposite of me." They loved hanging out with each other, even during a lengthy COVID quarantine in early 2021.

One memorable Wednesday in July of that year, they spent a whole day together, just the two of them. First, Jennifer braided Leanna's hair, something Leanna hadn't asked her to do for a couple of years. Then they drove up to nearby Riverside for lunch, came back home and lazed on the couch. Just them. Late that night, Leanna went out with a friend she hadn't seen in a while. The next morning, a scorcher, Jennifer dropped by Leanna's bedroom and told her she needed to close her window. After telling her a second time, Jennifer just walked in to close it herself.

"I was saying to myself, 'Of course she's moving.' I went to jiggle her shoulder or touch her. I saw the left side of her face. It looked like she was sleeping. But I knew." A seasoned dispatcher accustomed to fielding trauma calls from frantic, devastated parents, Jennifer started screaming and called 911.

Broken-hearted as she was – and still is – Jennifer was not naive. She was a mother who loved her daughter and tried to protect her.

> Kids screw around. Everybody knows that. When I was a teenager, I only messed with old-school minor marijuana. You can't do that now. I can't count how many times I said, "Whatever you decide to mess around with, you can't take a pill. You can never take a pill."

Leanna, a beautiful, green-eyed seventeen-year-old who "had her whole life in front of her, there were so many things she wanted to do," took a half tablet of what she and her friend thought was Percocet, a pain-killing drug. She died of fentanyl poisoning. "She had her retainers in."

Jennifer returned to work after just a month. Staying home wasn't going to change anything. "When I got back, I got a call from a mother whose daughter was overdosing in a pool." Though able to handle such calls by the book, a rapid succession of them – "just hearing the parents" – was too much for her. "I had to go home." Even without these types of calls, just being there was tough. Co-workers she had known for years wouldn't talk to her. Couldn't. They didn't know what to say or how to say it. She often felt isolated and alone. Six months passed and the July morning kept replaying in her head. "It's like a movie, like a reel. It never stops. I don't know when it will end."

FOR JENNIFER, THE LEAST appealing shift as a sheriff's dispatcher is the day shift. For one thing, she's not a morning person. And even though they call it the day shift, "it's just a bummer going to work in the dark and coming home in the dark." And there's this: "Morning hours are when people find their loved one, both old and young… who have passed away, are unresponsive or not waking up." But Jennifer signed up for a year-long stint on days anyway in case she decided to return to the RCC Evening Jazz Ensemble.

Just taking this seemingly modest step was daunting, sometimes to the point of paralysis. When her therapist asked what sort of things Jennifer liked to do for herself, playing trombone easily made the list. "She walked me through it. I got the horn out of the case. I put music on the stand. It took three weeks of therapy. It had nothing to do with Leanna, but it had everything to with my life before she died. Most times, I'd rather sit on the couch and crochet to calm myself instead of playing my horn. But I'm keeping my trombone out of the case because that makes it easier."

ON APRIL 18, 2022, the first night of a COVID-shortened semester for the jazz ensemble, I walked into the band room and saw Jennifer and the trombone her parents bought her decades ago sitting in the row between the saxes and the trumpets. I was surprised and elated. And struck by her courage. I unpacked my horn and sat down in my usual chair. Jennifer sat immediately to my right, home of the lead trombone. She protested that she was not yet in great trombone shape. Not much stamina. But the guys who had traded off on first trombone the prior semester just shrugged this off and passed her most of the lead parts.

As we played a succession of sight-unseen music, it was clear that her sight-reading chops had not deserted her. Neither had the purity of her tone, her confidence as she attacked the high notes and that innate ability to not just *play* the notes, but to put her stamp on the music. Following her was challenging and fun.

But not easy for her. "It was definitely difficult for me, a challenge the entire time … [but] I think making it to night band was a huge thing and it was progress. It's something I love being part of and I know it's good for my mental health for sure." Jennifer has moved from dispatch and trauma to personnel and recruitment and feels a huge sense of relief. "It's also bankers' hours," she wrote, "so there won't be any issues with attending night band."

When I read that, I was happy not just for Jennifer, but for myself, the band and Charlie, whose words rushed back to me. "She was one of the best lead players I ever had."

CHAPTER 10

Take Five

ONE MORNING IN the early 1990s, National Public Radio filled the brief gap between stories with a snippet of an oldie that dated back to the 1700s. This jazzy version of "Amazing Grace" surprised me, actually thrilled me, but I had no idea who had created it. I soon discovered this brilliant sound had been produced by just five instruments: two trumpets, one French horn, tuba and *trombone*. A brass quintet. The Canadian Brass, to be exact. A trombone could be part of a group that made this kind of music?

Within a few months, I was playing in a brass quintet. We called ourselves "Bach to the Future," putting our fan base (mainly our wives) on notice that we had no intention of confining our repertoire to a specific genre or a mere century. We were bellying up to an All-You-Can-Play musical buffet. It was plentiful and we were starving.

"We" included a tall, affable music educator (middle and high school) who once led the Riverside City College Evening Jazz Ensemble. Jerry Lees played first trumpet. A CPA with a vast knowledge of the SoCal avocado industry played second trumpet. Kirk Stitt blended a bumper crop of common sense with a jolly sense of humor. Our French horn player, Bob Bell, was a second-grade teacher who had performed professionally in Europe and Mexico. Tuba players were tough to find and hard to keep. But our turnstile of tubists frequently featured Curtiss Allen Jr., a middle school music teacher who made us Christmas-and-Easter fixtures at his San Bernardino church whose congregation feasted on music.

We tried to rehearse each week, sometimes in my Riverside living room within earshot of Guido and later Seymour, our official rehearsal dogs. We began to amass a library, purchasing the Canadian Brass arrangement of "Amazing Grace," of course, and much more. Some music was familiar: Scott Joplin's "The Entertainer," Glenn Miller's "In the Mood," Bernstein's *West Side Story*. I knew Jean-Joseph Mouret's fanfare long before I ever played it. *"Rondeau"* was the theme to TV's *Masterpiece Theater.*

But most of the stuff was new to me. Bach's "Air on a G String" was as beautiful as the title was misleading. There was no air. The slow tempo left me gasping for oxygen. (The "G string" refers to a violin, so you can get your mind out of the gutter.) We also played Mozart, Brahms and Handel and worked up hymns, early music, Christmas carols, marches and even a Hanukkah medley. We even bought music we never played.

As we passed around *Fiddler on the Roof*, Bob Bell grew clammy and pale. While in Amsterdam, he spent two years playing French horn for *Fiddler* every night and twice on Sundays. By the time he flew to Mexico City for his new job with the Mexico National Symphony, his body had rejected the music. When he entered the city's airport terminal to the piped-in strains of "If I Were a Rich Man," Post-Traumatic *Fiddler* Disorder kicked in and never left. We retired this masterpiece without playing a note.

Though Bach to the Future was hardly an overnight sensation, or even a sensation, we started getting gigs and spent much of what we earned on music. We played at malls, street festivals, museums, a fancy furniture store and churches, including at a ceremony for the Bishop of the Diocese of San Bernardino. We sometimes suited up in tuxedos and white tennis shoes, a nod to our Canadian Brass idols. We played for anyone who called to hire us, even if they weren't quite sure what they were hiring. Potential clients frequently asked, "How many are there in your quintet?"

Some gigs were impossible to forget. After playing a nice tight set at a downtown Riverside festival, I hung around for the next show, enthralled by the exotic talent. A dour newspaper pal standing beside me placed our own performance in an unflattering context. "You were the warm-up for a bird act." I couldn't deny that the crowd swelled after we left the stage.

We arrived right on time for a Christmas gig at an Orange County shopping mall, having stuttered through rush-hour freeway traffic. As we unloaded our gear and brushed off our tuxes, one of our revolving-door tuba players muttered, "I hope I didn't forget my mouthpiece." We played the first hour as a quartet.

This Orange County excursion highlighted what every musician knows: there is more to playing music than playing music. When to rehearse, what to wear to a gig, what time to show up, where to park and remembering to bring a mouthpiece are all part of the package. For years after that Orange County snafu, I found myself pulling off the road on the way to a performance, popping the trunk and opening my case to make sure I hadn't forgotten my mouthpiece. It was just another symptom of my long-time affliction: Charlie Maxwell Syndrome.

Charlie Maxwell played baseball for the Detroit Tigers. My only childhood memory of him goes back to a Tigers–Yankees game when I smirked as only a snotty ten-year-old Yankees fan could smirk when "Easy Out" Maxwell came to bat. After he clobbered his game-winning homer, I felt as if the baseball had rocketed out of the stadium, pierced my radio and lodged in my gut. I was devastated. But I also realized snotty smirking had been a grave error and immediately began to expect only the worst possible outcomes. This helped me blossom into a chronic worrier who took nothing for granted, left nothing to chance.

I became known as "Mother," routinely phoning my fellow quints to remind them about rehearsals and gigs, when to show up and when to change their underwear. After a wildfire prevented one player (and his music) from making a gig, I proposed that all our music be placed in the custody of one person, namely me. This idea didn't live long enough to be pronounced dead on arrival. I realized I was turning into Al Haig who famously (and incorrectly) declared, "I'm in control here," after President Reagan was shot. I knew I had to let go. It was the hardest thing someone with Charlie Maxwell Syndrome ever had to do.

IT WOULD BE UNTHINKABLE for some music groups to even consider changing personnel. John, Paul, George and Ringo were, in a musical sense, Siamese quadruplets. When they separated, the Beatles expired. Peter, Paul & Mary could never have become Peter, Paul & Marge. But other bands seemed to change personnel as often as designers adjusted hem lines. Santana, the rock band formed in 1966 and still playing in 2022, had gone through at least sixty-eight members. The Canadian Brass, formed in 1970, has had twenty-five different members. As a new millennium dawned, Bach to the Future, not entirely immune to the tension and friction common among some groups, entered an Era of Musical Chairs. We became BrassWorks and welcomed our first woman member.

Lisa Forster had already been playing trumpet in UC Riverside's orchestra and jazz band. She came to BrassWorks with "high chops" (the piccolo trumpet part in the Beatles' "Penny Lane" was well within her range) and the unerring eye of a UCR lab researcher. Before long, our library and rehearsals were undergoing intense scrutiny. She thought we were wasting too much time preparing for gigs. She wanted us to be ready when the phone rang. That way, we could spend more rehearsal time working up new music. It was hard to disagree with her. So we didn't.

Other changes swirled about the quintet as well. Job pressures, family obligations, personality clashes, new opportunities and other forms of "life" led to departures and arrivals. A fine tuba player got in big trouble with the law. Poof! He was gone. Another tubist was excited to play gigs, but skipped rehearsals. Without notice. He was dumbfounded when we cut him loose. Without notice. When certain passages proved too difficult for a French horn player, he simply didn't play them. And there was The Starbucks Incident.

Days before an evening gig at The Back Street, a popular outdoor Riverside restaurant, a fine young tuba player studying in LA informed us that he could not make the performance. But he assured us that he had found a sub. The general rule for "finding a sub" is to line up someone with equal or superior ability. This tuba player took a somewhat different approach. Ordering a beverage at Starbucks, he struck up a conversation with a young barista that seemed to go something like this:

> Our Tuba Player: "Double latte, please. I play tuba."
>
> Barista: "So do I. Croissant?"
>
> OTP: "Biscotti. Can you sub for me in two days?"
>
> Barista: *"Oooompahhhh!!!!"*

The Starbucks Incident. Cartoon by Philip Neuman.

The barista arrived at my house for a rehearsal and departed after one-and-a-half tunes. He had walked into an awkward and, especially for him, unfair situation. By this time, around 2009, Lisa was playing in a jazz band directed by a well-known SoCal band leader/arranger, and had compiled a list of possible quintet subs. As the rest of us shifted our weight and examined our shoes, Lisa made a cold call to Orange County. A few evenings later, as the four of us arranged chairs and music stands on a small stage in The Back Street's cozy garden courtyard, in strode a six-four, square-jawed gentleman with a tuba strapped to his back. His name was Charlie Warren. Chaz.

We began our first set with an arrangement of Duke Ellington's "Ain't Got That Swing," a tune that had become our musical equivalent of comfort food. It erased the jitters. The trumpets and the French horn don't play a note until the fourth measure. The trombone makes an appearance in the first measure, but not until the second beat. The first beat is the sole property of the tuba. When Chaz hit that previously nondescript G, I felt a tingle. I'd never heard it played that way and the next few notes packed the same punch. These weren't over-the-top blats. This was more like a craftsman laying down a solid oak floor for the rest of us. His presence snapped us to attention, making us more cohesive and energetic. "You could just feel that he was so connected to what was going on," Lisa Forster recalled. "He even shifted to look at each player as the lead moved around the group."

It wasn't the first time I'd caught myself marveling at the magic of music: Someone you've never met – and in some cases a stranger you will never talk to or see again – unpacks an instrument and, with barely a word spoken, joins a musical conversation that flows so effortlessly that a listener would assume the group had played together for years.

As we packed up after our final tune, Chaz popped the question that would change everything. "When's the next gig?" Though we didn't know it at the time, we had just spent two hours with a self-described "Quintet Head."

Charlie "Chaz" Warren, tuba. PHOTO BY CARLOS PUMA.

CHAZ WAS BORN into a culture of music, performance and reptiles in 1952. Hometown: Newport Beach, California. His mother, who eventually became a "self-proclaimed housewife," once auditioned for a vaudeville show in LA and got the part – until they discovered the young acrobat was only thirteen. Chaz's father grew up in the SoCal desert near the Salton Sea. The nearest piano teacher was seventy miles away. But Chaz's grandmother insisted that her kids take lessons, which meant road trips to San Diego in a Model T Ford. One outing coincided with a contest sponsored by the San Diego Zoo to see who could bring in the most rattlesnakes. Chaz's dad, then nine, knew rattlers lounged on desert roads at night, soaking up heat. Armed with a forked stick and gunny sacks, he and his kid brother bagged and boxed enough rattlers to fill the trunk with a hissing choir.

Chaz's father became a proficient pianist and introduced his son to the world he would explore and occupy for decades to come. "Listen to that tuba player," his dad would say. Then he'd light into the piano, demonstrating exactly what the tuba had just done. "He taught me bass lines. He was kind of my tutor with Dixieland."

Chaz wanted to play sax. But his grandmother – the same grandma who hauled that trunkful of snakes to San Diego – wouldn't hear of it. There are millions of sax players, she told him. Play bass and you'll always get work. This astonished him. "Get paid for playing music?"

He was tall for his age and his school music teacher took full advantage. "My jaw dropped when I saw it," recalled Chaz, who didn't even know what "it" was. But the fifth-grader quickly learned to play the string bass and went on to play it in high school. Mindful of the challenges of schlepping such an instrument in a marching band, he learned to play tuba as he strutted on the gridiron. Then it was on to Cal State Long Beach, where Chaz immersed himself in civil engineering and construction. And nearly drowned. "Calculus and chemistry were kicking me where it hurt." When he took an aptitude test, hoping it would point him toward a less painful path, the results came back "Musical Performer." Chaz had never heard of such a thing but, "I pretty much quit everything and went back to junior college and started as a music major."

Chaz was in his mid-twenties when the combined wisdom of the aptitude test and his grandmother became apparent. "Nobody's going to play tuba," predicted a friend who told Chaz about an audition for a band consisting of a washboard, banjo, clarinet and tuba. Chaz auditioned and became a member of Disneyland's Main Street

BrassWorks: *Mark Prather, trumpet; Dan Bernstein, trombone; Chaz Warren, tuba; Bob Bell, French horn; Lisa Forster, trumpet.* Photo by Carlos Puma.

Maniacs. That 1978 seasonal gig opened the Magic Kingdom to Chaz and his tuba, string bass and bass saxophone for the next forty years.

In 1997, Chaz landed his "favorite job ever" after reporting to the Disneyland Hotel and auditioning for a spit-polished quintet suddenly in need of a tuba. He became a member of the Bellhops. When the hotel underwent renovations, they became the Hard Hats or Splattertones. During Christmas season, the brass quintet morphed into the Mistletones. The only downside was acute abdominal pain. "They were the funniest guys I ever played with. I'd come home with stomach aches from laughing. They were extremely lighthearted, but fantastic musicians."

By the time Chaz arrived at The Back Street as an emergency sub for a barista, the Bellhops had morphed into the Pacific Coast Horns (PCH), a high-performance brass quintet. He also had become a prolific and generous arranger of brass quintet music. Much later, when I told him how thrilled we were that night when he asked about the next gig, he replied, "I was hoping you'd call me back." I had to know why.

"Here I am, stepping in with a group that already knows all the tunes. If anyone has to think, it's me. It's a challenge." Plus, he was already making that dreadful commute from Anaheim to Riverside, where he taught tuba at Riverside City College. And there was something else that appealed to Chaz that had nothing but perhaps everything to do with music.

Tall, strong and athletic, Chaz was a high-school standout in water polo and swimming and hoped to make an even bigger splash in junior college until a friend talked him into going out for crew. He did Olympics-caliber well. Big-time colleges with elite teams recruited him. "Crew is the ultimate ensemble sport. Perfect timing, super smooth application of all your strength, developing a synchronized swing among the rowers." Perfect chemistry is vital, noted Chaz, because "if disaster strikes, you're in the water."

Playing in a brass quintet in a flat, dry living room is somewhat less hazardous, but developing that "synchronized swing" is no less challenging. In his eye-opening non-fiction book, *Canyon Dreams: A Basketball Season on the Navajo Nation*, Michael Powell catches the high school coach in a moment of frustration: "I love the sport because it takes five people playing together like musicians. What's so difficult about that to understand?"

It's not a stretch to flip the script: a brass quintet takes five people playing together like hoopsters. Everyone is exposed. There's no place to hide. "Everybody has an integral part to play," said Chaz. "You're pretty much it whatever you're doing, be it harmony, melody or bass line."

"Pretty much it" pretty much describes it. I was no longer playing in a trombone section. I *was* the trombone section. If the trombone had the melody, I played it. But it didn't feel like a high-wire act because there is a unique intimacy in a quintet. Just five of us, all pulling in the same direction in the same boat, tuba at the stern with the rest of us, sitting two abreast, facing each other. No life jackets.

IN THE JAZZ band, I enjoyed an unobstructed if largely unhelpful view of the back of sax players' heads. That was okay because I could gaze over or between them and see the director. In BrassWorks, there was no director, which threatened to make us directionless even as we tried to pull in the same direction. We had to find ways to communicate. We kept our eyes peeled and our ears open (only our noses were allowed to take a breather). The horn player and I locked eyeballs a split second before plunging into harmony to make sure we were in sync. All eyes were riveted on whoever was responsible for giving a cue to enter, exit or stop holding a particularly long note. We had to be alert because, as Chaz observed, even during a performance "things are changing at every instant and performers are adapting to every changing nuance." This is what he was looking for that first evening at The Back Street: How would we adapt?

"I enjoy playing with groups that have a passion for the music, not just messing around. I saw that in BrassWorks. People who are really enjoying it, communicating with each other in a very relaxed fashion. Everybody was cheering for each other. Oftentimes in professional groups, people are kind of cutthroat and have their own agenda. I didn't see any of that. I just saw positive."

With Chaz, it only became more positive. The chemistry was notable for the absence of friction. Working conditions included the laughter-related abdominal discomfort. If it was Tuesday at 5 p.m., we convened in my living room (no reminder phone calls necessary), moved furniture, put up music stands and braced for random cameos by the latest rehearsal dog. When we had a gig, we ran our sets, now opening with Chaz's arrangement of "Kiss the Girl" from Disney's *Little Mermaid*. When we didn't, we tackled new music. Chaz, who called himself our Taskmaster, often arranged music with individual "BrassWorkers" in mind. "Moondance" begins with an edge and relaxes into a gentle swing for the trombone solo – in a user-friendly key.

Chaz had it right: We *were* cheering for each other, trying to achieve that "synchronized swing," despite obstacles large and small. Too often, I tested the group's patience by playing about a half-beat ahead of the pack. (I attributed this to my rushin' heritage.) Many songs required intense work between our weekly sessions. But we had an unstated pact. We didn't want to let each other down.

Not long after joining BrassWorks, Chaz asked if anyone could sing. Soon, Chaz and I and dazzling trumpet player Mark Prather – a second-grade teacher and alumnus of the elite North Texas State University One O'Clock Lab Band – were belting out parodies to "*Bei Mir Bis Du Shein*" (we sang "The Bear Missed the Train") and "The Three Caballeros" from the Disney film with the same title. During a holiday concert at UC Riverside, we sang a seasonal version (confession: I wrote it) of "Three Caballeros." The first verse noted the politically incorrect peril of wishing someone a "Merry Christmas." The second verse provided a solution.

Say Ho-ho-ho-ho!
We have some other choices
Right here in our voices,
Though we might sound odd.

Although we are gringos,
We have other lingos.
We wish our amigos
¡Feliz Navidad!

Chaz blizzarded us with masterpieces, from his arrangements of the latest Disney tunes to his inspired concoction of "Concert in a Box" – snippets of thirty classics including Tchaikovsky's "March Slav," "Yankee Doodle," "She'll Be Coming 'Round the Mountain," Sousa's "Liberty Bell" march and "Peter and the Wolf" and, of course, a Christmas carol. At gigs, we took turns calling a song, producing unscripted sets that lurched from "*The Music Man* Medley" to themes from *The Simpsons* and "Mario Brothers" to the Tijuana Brass and the Beatles. If we had ever played a Broadway show, "Magnificent 7" would have stopped it. Every audience loved "Mag 7" – even if they had to ask what it was. And it was a kick to watch jaws drop and eyes pop as young people listened in startled disbelief when a quintet comprised mainly of aging baby boomers launched into a composition inspired by a hot new talent who had dubbed herself Lady Gaga.

Tio's Tacos, a downtown Riverside Mexican restaurant, was one of our favorite gig spots. Its sprawling grounds offered a whimsical landscape of sculptures and structures crafted from stuff other people had thrown away: a small church constructed almost entirely of beer bottles; towering humanoids created from plastic milk jugs, dead keyboards and generations of discarded Barbies. On gentle spring and summer evenings, we set up on the restaurant owner's front porch overlooking the courtyard restaurant and serenaded diners, including friends and relatives or, if a quintet can claim to have such a thing, groupies. At Tio's, we played for tips and food. Other gigs got each of us $150. Great gigs, $200. We kept our day jobs.

Mark Prather (l), Dan & Chaz Warren singing at a quintet gig at Tio's Tacos in Riverside, June 2011. PHOTO BY ROGER MYERS.

We played a beautiful wedding at the Los Angeles Athletic Club, a somber world of hard wood, soft leather and deep pockets. We played a Friday night concert at Riverside's stunningly picturesque citrus park, known for its undulating groves of fruit-bearing trees. There was a substitute French horn player that night – an Orange County import and Chaz's close friend. About halfway through the evening, he told us about a gig that would be perfectly suited to our music.

Lisa Forster, Dan Bernstein, Mark Prather playing while not playing.
Photo by Carlos Puma.

For the next two summers we played at an ocean-front home in Manhattan Beach – a sprawling fortress of teak and glass built to replace the two ocean-fronters the owners had torn down. Both of these spare-no-expense parties included dinner, dancing and costumes created by handsomely paid designers. Fittingly, the first party's theme was "Gatsby," echoing the opulent excess of the devil-may-care 1920s. Guests sparkled with their slinky gowns, flappers, foot-long cigarette holders, felt fedoras and flashy suspenders. I tried my best to blend in by repeatedly viewing a YouTube video in which two gentlemen in a South Carolina men's store demonstrated the art of tying a bow tie. The second party had a more down-home theme related to farming and crops. Our "costumes" featured jeans, bandanas, cowboy hats. If there'd been a prize for "Ripest Costume," it would have gone to the couple dressed as halves of the same avocado, pit included. During slow dances, the human avocado formed a most perfect union.

If I had to place BrassWorks gigs on a cultural spectrum, that Manhattan Beach party palace would occupy one end and Sherman Indian High School the other. This "off-reservation" Riverside boarding school, one of about twenty-five in the U.S., dated back to 1892, serving students from nearly eighty tribes throughout the U.S. When the school hired BrassWorks to play at its commencement, we sat in the balcony, watching the pageantry and taking in student speeches that shimmered with pride and hope. As the grads received their diplomas, we hoisted our instruments and played the old standby: "Pomp & Circumstance." It took me back to my own graduation, when I played the same song over and over again as my classmates marched across the stage. Now as then, the risk of getting lost in the repetitive loop was real. But sitting almost side by side in the upper reaches of the auditorium, I reminded myself that we weren't just playing for the students. We were playing for *each* of them. I tried to envision that at the precise moment a new graduate finally grasped that slice of parchment, she or he would hear us playing "Pomp and Circumstance" just for them. Much later, I wondered why Sherman Indian School decided to hire BrassWorks to play almost nothing but "Pomp & Circumstance," a military march composed for an English king. Native Americans have their own rich traditions and ceremonies that mark and honor life's milestones. I have a feeling someone at the school thought of this much sooner than I did. When we played "Pomp & Circumstance" again the next year, it was our Sherman Indian High School swan song.

And then it was over. Not overnight, but this page-turning, five-year chapter of BrassWorks had reached its climax. Mark Prather packed up his lovely sound, especially on flugelhorn, and moved to California Gold Rush country. Chris Watts, a tireless and inspiring Riverside elementary school teacher and our premier go-to trumpet sub, stepped right in. When Chris and Chaz played in BrassWorks, we were the only quintet in America featuring two musicians with perfect impressions of Bullwinkle the Moose. But Lisa soon retired from the UC Riverside lab and moved to Northern California. Chaz gravitated back to Orange County, where he had built a studio and regularly hosted quintet sessions. Julie Quinones, our young, exquisitely talented French horn player, landed a full-time teaching job far from Riverside. I retired and began spending summers in Central Oregon, where I kept up my chops by playing at, well, a dump.

When this chapter of BrassWorks began, Chaz wasn't measuring us against the Canadian Brass, the Pacific Coast Horns, the LA Lakers or any other quintet. He measured us against ourselves: people grinding through day jobs or college classes and still trying to produce what Chaz called "the best product" possible. If the yardstick sometimes seemed to extend beyond our reach, it only made us try harder and savor the moments when we finally caught up and played with that elusive yet so satisfying synchronized swing. It is astonishing to reflect that this chapter unfolded after such a chance encounter. If a tuba player hadn't walked into a Starbucks, all of what happened next might never have happened at all.

Chapter 11

Penny Lane

Lisa Forster might have opted for a career in music if she hadn't seen what she couldn't unsee in that Volvo. She was in college at the time, the principal trumpet in the UC Riverside Orchestra. She was playing the high, hard stuff: Handel's "The Trumpet Shall Sound," on a piccolo trumpet, the tiniest and possibly the most difficult-to-deal-with instrument in the trumpet family. At times, she had that euphoric experience of playing flawlessly before a large audience and feeling no pressure, not a single twitch of nerves. She felt like she was the only one in the concert hall, floating among the notes that shot out of her instrument with such piercing clarity. As the athletes say, she was in a zone.

Lisa Forster, trumpet. Photo by Carlos Puma.

Lisa was born in Riverside in 1960, one of two girls in a family of four. Her mom was a registered nurse. Her dad was a machinist, a lifelong "tinkerer" and owner of a downtown bar next to the bus depot. The family lived in Highgrove, a "citrus belt suburb" awash in open space and citrus orchards with plenty of room to build forts, ride the neighbor's horse, pick blackberries, even make go-carts. There wasn't enough family money for an allowance, but from elementary through high school, Lisa and her sister each earned a dollar an hour packaging nylons in a neighbor's home. Eventually, her parents saved enough to buy a piano.

When her mother's sisters came down from Montana, they'd sit down at that piano and bang out what they called honky-tonk. Before long, her mom would break out the accordion she'd had since she was a child. But when the sisters left, Lisa's mother went back to playing what she loved most: classical music. Lisa's dad was hooked on the big bands. The little house in Highgrove was bursting with so much music that the matriarch's edict surprised no one: Lisa and her sister had to take piano lessons for five years. After that, they could quit and pick their own instrument. Five years later, Lisa picked the trumpet. "I always loved the soaring trumpet lines on several of mom's albums," especially "What Kind of Fool Am I" by the Mantovani Orchestra. And then there was the trumpet itself. "I thought to myself, 'How hard can it be? There are only three valves.'"

For the first two weeks, on orders from the band director, the ambitious Highgrove Elementary School fifth grader only played the mouthpiece. Miraculously, her parents didn't evict her. She soared through middle and high schools like a chord progression, with tension resolving to triumph. She expanded her range, improved her tone, started private lessons, had her first exposure to jazz and left the spacious confines of Riverside County to play in honor bands. She was the first girl in the entire middle school band and the only female playing lead *and* solos at Riverside's North High School. "Our neighborhood was small and mainly boys, so we [Lisa and her sister] grew up as competitive tomboys." She would also grow up to be a member of the UC Riverside's national championship volleyball team.

When Lisa started at UCR, she decided it was time to quit playing her trumpet and focus on school. It was an irreversible decision that lasted all of nine months and ended with a phone call. Lisa had gone to high school with a girl whose dad conducted the university's orchestra. He knew all about Lisa and knew he wasn't happy with his lead trumpet player. He offered the chair to Lisa. She played in the orchestra for the next twenty years.

During that first decade, she played nothing but classical music, learning the various trumpets the music demanded. She took lessons from the university's resident trumpet teacher who was also a professional performing musician. One day, she caught a glimpse of the interior of his Volvo and instantly made a career decision. The back seat was appointed with a tuxedo – and a pillow. The image shocked her. "It steered me clear of going into music professionally, especially classical. There simply weren't enough jobs; the competition was ferocious."

As a UCR graduate, Lisa found herself in the doldrums of a job she didn't like when she received a call from yet another UC Riverside professor with yet another offer. Not for an orchestra full of musicians, but a lab full of insects. While in college Lisa had worked in the Department of Entomology. Now, she was back and would eventually run the lab that raised and deployed the natural enemies of pests that killed citrus and threatened to wipe out an entire industry.

Through all the pest research and analysis, the tracking and trapping, the international travel to Vietnam, China, Thailand and South Africa, Lisa made time for music. Sometimes, it was inside the cinder-block building that housed temperature chambers for experiments, sometimes a hotel closet or a remote citrus orchard. It didn't matter. Lisa found the time and place to practice her trumpet. When UCR's orchestra or jazz band rehearsed, she was right there in her chair. She began studying with Bobby Shew. The SoCal master of jazz trumpet and flugelhorn helped her become more "efficient" at playing those high jazz lead lines so she could "compete with the guys." When it came time to compete, she was ready.

A friend took her to Orange County to watch a rehearsal of a jazz band directed by Tom Kubis, well known for his arrangements of big-band music. After her friend "bragged me up," the trumpet section, which included a gentleman who'd played the Academy Awards the night before, invited her to sit in. A few years later, she joined the Tom Kubis Monday Night Band and eventually became the lead trumpet player.

"She was so interesting," recalled Kubis, "in that she was wonderful at playing in the brass quintet area, but had this amazing ability to sit in a big band and play lead or any other chair… We had so many guys who wanted to sit on the lead chair…but she was the better player." He remembers Lisa as a woman who was humble and kind and possessed with a "keen desire to improve. She was a staple in our trumpet section, the best of the best in our ensemble."

It was no different as the lead trumpet in BrassWorks. "Here it is," she'd say, setting a tempo or demonstrating a tricky rhythm that was befuddling the rest of us. No one worked harder than Lisa, but there was no harm in trying because it usually paid off. Chaz Warren, our Taskmaster, had given us a piece called "Tirade of the Wooden Tuba." His version of "March of the Wooden Soldiers" featured a piccolo trumpet and tuba sharing the lead. Recalled Lisa: "After playing it and putting it away, I don't think Chaz ever thought we would perform it. I remember the four of us working on it on our own, without him knowing." During a rehearsal, when it was her turn to call a tune, Lisa called *that* tune. "How fun it was to see his eyes light up after we finished." We eventually performed it, with Lisa showcasing what Tom Kubis called "that genuine fire in her playing."

Always looking for a way to take "every advantage from my equipment every day, not just the day I bought it or when I washed it," Lisa tapped into the "tinker gene" she'd inherited from her dad. She trimmed foam test-tube stoppers to size, drenched them in rubbing alcohol, wrung them out and blew them through her horn. The result: a product that dried out a clean horn and mouthpiece after they'd been played and kept them clean. BlowDry Brass continues to enjoy steady sales.

In 2014, Lisa retired and moved to Cottonwood, way up in Northern California, to be close to her mother, sister and brother-in-law. Today, she maintains a large spread of land, fishes and plays at her church. When she looks through the rearview mirror, she sees a life lived without a tuxedo and a pillow and regrets. "I am still happy with my decision not to pursue a career in music. I think it would have been too stressful, and I did have a very fulfilling career in research – a completely different world from music."

But music still sings to her. She has gone back to the woodshed, reviving the high chops that raised so many eyebrows and perked-up so many ears. It hasn't been easy, but considering the trumpet only has three valves, how hard could it be?

Chapter 12

Seventy-six Trombones

Actually, I only have four. One friend has fifteen trombones. I've played with two people who have at least a dozen trumpets between them. Another has eight tubas. There's a story behind everyone one of these instruments. There is always a story.

The relationship between musicians and their instruments may appear to be strictly transactional: I'll do my job, you do yours. But it's not that simple. These liaisons are layered with feelings and emotions. As Tommy Dorsey played, "I'm Getting Sentimental Over You," who was he really serenading? His audience? His lover? His trombone?

"I think we all have intense feelings, one way or another, for our horns," said Charlie Richard, who is among the very best saxophone players in Southern California. He owns and is expected to be able to *play* soprano, alto, tenor and baritone saxes. All are "very fine instruments, likely better than I deserve." Think about that. Charlie is an immensely talented musician. Yet among the intense feelings he has for *his* instruments is a suspicion that they're too good for him. These relationships are almost human.

The trombone I play the least is the first one I ever played. The Cannibal is actually only *half* of the first trombone I ever had. The half that I still have is the shiny brass bell, part of the Olds student model I started out with in the late 1950s, in fourth grade. The bell's engraving says it is an Ambassador, manufactured in Fullerton, California. The Cannibal's slide once belonged to an Oregon friend who stopped playing when he was a kid. It glided much more smoothly than the sandpapery slide on my Ambassador. When my friend's dad announced that the abandoned trombone had to go, I gladly took half of it. I play the Cannibal at select venues, most notably as a volunteer at a transfer station, or dump, located in a national forest in Central Oregon. When I'm not standing in a dumpster, stomping down other people's trash, I assemble the Cannibal, power up my hotdog-sized speaker and, backed by my digital band, entertain the customers.

Before I retired, I had a long, exclusive relationship with my King 3-B Silver Sonic, the trombone my parents bought me when I was in high school. Its serial number revealed it to be a child of the '60s and it truly was as beautiful and innocent as a flower child. The silver bell glistened and the slide slid ever so slickly. The sound, however, was only as good as I could make it. At times, it reminded me of a summer-camp incident where I drew the fastest horse for a race. When I didn't even come close to winning, my fellow campers, a jealous and petty lot, sneered that I rode a horse I didn't deserve. Of course, they were right. I often felt the same way about my Silver Sonic as I played it through high school, college and far into balding adulthood.

The Silver Sonic was my all-purpose horn, except at the dump. It never crossed my mind to become anything more than a two-trombone wonder. But one night, a fellow trombone player in the jazz band, suggested that a smaller horn would be a better fit in our section. By smaller he meant skinnier, not shorter. Narrower tubing. A smaller bore that would brighten the sound and put the higher notes within easier reach. In short, he wanted me to get what is sometimes known as a pea shooter.

THERE ARE MANY ways to shop for the perfect musical instrument. Mark Prather, who played in BrassWorks, routinely arrived at rehearsals with a shiny, previously unseen object swaddled in an unscarred case. When someone invariably shouted, "Another new one!," Mark replied with a sheepish shrug. He didn't actually buy trumpets. He auditioned them, frequently sending them back, ordering something else and sending *that* back. He was searching for "the Holy Grail, or as some of us say 'unicorns.' We dream of finding a 'closet queen' that was bought new and stashed away for fifty years, only to make a dramatic appearance in all its pristine glory."

Alex Henderson, who plays trombone in the RCC jazz band when not on tour with Big Bad Voodoo Daddy, has a trombone for low notes, a "big" horn for the classical stuff, a pea shooter for jazz. All very practical. But his double-digit inventory has also been swelled by impulse and emotion. He has purchased King trombones for "ridiculous bargains" during chance visits to pawn shops. A trombone languishing in a repair shop turned out to be a prototype built for a true trombone legend, Frank Rosolino. "I had to have it just because Frank Rosolino touched it." He bought a used Yamaha not only "because it was a beautiful rose brass color" just like the one his first trombone teacher had, but because it turned out the be the "main ax" of a famous Salsa trombonist. Reasoned Alex, "If I buy the horn, maybe I can sound like him!"

By comparison, my search for a pea shooter was short, sweet and (small) boring. I went online, found a trombone website, spotted an ad with a couple of photos and bought the thing without ever touching it. The gentleman who sold it to me wasn't famous, at least not that I knew of, and made no claim that his instrument had ever been played or even fondled by a legend, dead or alive. He just said it was a great jazz trombone and he was only selling it because he had bought another great jazz trombone. But here's what sealed the deal: It was a King and it resided in New Orleans.

The King 2-B arrived in a sturdy, nondescript black case, signaling that this was no fancy-pants instrument. It weighed less than my 3-B Silver Sonic. The slide was uninjured and buttery smooth. Its overall appearance – dull, honey-colored brass accented by scratches, dings, pits and expanses of chipped or missing lacquer – revealed that it had paid its dues. On closer look, however, it was beautiful. The bell was engraved with tiers of Art Nouveau flourishes. "2-B" appears beneath the first burst of painstakingly engraved feathers. Beneath those, 'KING" and finally a mysterious "Chberg," which turned out to stand for Charles H. Berg, whose company, White & Berg, manufactured the first King trombone in 1894. The serial number on my New Orleans trombone shows that it was born between 1950 and 1955. A fellow baby boomer. And as it turned out, a first-rate jazz trombone.

I WAS SET: 2-B for the jazz band and not 2-B (the Silver Sonic) for the quintet. But I wasn't listening as carefully as Chaz Warren, the Quintet

Head/Taskmaster, who one day suggested that a bigger horn would be a better fit for BrassWorks. By that he meant a *larger* bore whose sound would blend seamlessly with the tuba and the French horn.

Soon, I was roaming the vast Anaheim Convention Center during the NAMM (National Association of Music Merchants) annual trade show that showcases the very latest in guitar picks, violin strings, plastic instruments from China, mutant amplifiers and everything else, including glistening trombones, large and small. I tested and re-tested and eventually settled on a gorgeous German-made trombone that met Chaz's large-bore specs but wasn't too heavy for someone in my demographic: aging. Mission accomplished, I decided to reward myself by sampling smaller trombones just to compare them with what I already had. I'd even brought my mouthpiece, which I couldn't use to test that German-made wonder because it was much too small.

I picked an exhibit booth that displayed plenty of normal-sized trombones, selected a beauty, inserted my mouthpiece and, conscious of bystanders, instructed myself to start with a warm, rich sound. But nothing happened. I mean *nothing*. Either I had picked up a defective instrument or someone had played it and damaged it before I got there. There were plenty of trombones to choose from so I picked another. Again, nothing. I rushed to a competitor's booth and tried *their* trombones but could barely blow air through the horn. I began to panic. Had I somehow damaged my lips and mouth muscles by playing those gigantic trombones? Before I called Chaz (after all, this was *his* idea), I carefully inspected my mouthpiece. It had not undergone such scrutiny since I nervously surrendered it at the San Francisco airport the first day commercial flights resumed after 9/11. But even as I examined it, I grumbled, "As if anything could go wrong with a hunk of steel." Convinced I was wasting my time, I pointed the mouthpiece toward the ceiling, expecting to be drenched in a fluorescent glare. Instead, I was blinded by darkness, which got me thinking. NAMM shows are head-crushingly loud. Music and "music" blast away like artillery. I had learned that the hard way and this time came prepared. Without even calling Chaz, I managed to extract the foreign object that had become lodged in the shaft of my hunk of steel. It was one of the Tylenol tablets I'd dropped into the same pocket where I'd deposited my mouthpiece. I picked up the nearest normal trombone and tried once again, not caring if I produced the most flatulent blat known to man. I just remember that whatever came out sounded as if it had descended from the heavens.

OVER THE YEARS, California has devolved from the Golden State to the Golden-Brown State to the Red Flag Warning State. Drought, wildfires and evacuations have become the nightmarish realities of the California Dream. Which raises a question that probes the intensity musicians feel for their instruments: If you were ordered to evacuate and could take just one instrument with you, which would it be?

Charlie Richard, the college prof, band director, composer and owner of a slew of reed instruments, would rescue the saxophone his mom and dad bought him for Christmas back when he was a community college student. It was a used sax, a Selmer Mark VI if you're scoring at home, on sale in Hollywood. Charlie's teacher talked it up to his parents. "My instrument is fabulous." Leave it behind in a fire? Not a chance.

Mark Prather, who has auditioned his share of trumpets, has "a very expensive flugelhorn made in Spain that I'd better grab first." But not just because it's worth a lot of dough. "It's really the horn I want to grow old with. It reads my mind and turns it into music."

My choice is a no-brainer, too. I'd tuck my King 3-B Silver Sonic into its coffin case and, along with my wife and sheepdogs, off we'd go. It's a horn with a history: *our* history.

We once road-tripped together from California to Arkansas just to play during a college football game. And drove through a New Mexico blizzard on a trip from Denver to Pasadena to play in the Rose Parade and an even more memorable football game.

I hung a high F on that horn in a high-school concert and am still trying to duplicate that feat. I held it in my hands as I got slugged in the knee by Tasso Harris, my trombone teacher. Before a trip, I locked it in a closet so no one could steal it – and forgot where I hid the key. Hiring a locksmith is a little-known aspect of trombone ownership.

I have *parented* this trombone: bathed it, oiled it, taken it to various trombone doctors and showered it with accessories: cup mutes, straight mutes, bucket mutes, a trombone stand and even a toilet plunger that has never (to my knowledge) been immersed in a bowl.

But at times, I have treated this trombone unkindly. During a rehearsal for a Stanford halftime show, I sprinted to the center of the football field along with a million other instrument-wielding bandmates. The idea was to scatter right back out into another formation. But I collided with someone. Rather, my trombone did, damaging the most delicate part of the instrument: the slide. I've had it tweaked and re-tweaked but it has never been quite the same.

I benched my 3-B it in favor of that hot little jazz number from New Orleans. I eventually felt terribly guilty and brought it back when I noticed other Silver Sonics popping up in the trombone section.

Not that long ago, I gave my beloved trombone a much-needed bath and left it soaking in warm, soapy water just a smidge too long. It brought back haunting memories of my teenage years when I scrubbed our cream-colored station wagon with steel wool as I prepped it for a date. (My parents were too dumbfounded to be angry.) The prolonged soaking stripped away the lacquer, transforming my horn from a Silver Sonic to a Splotchy Sonic. But if that evacuation order ever arrived, I wouldn't hesitate to grab it and run because (with sincere apologies to Messrs. Lerner and Loewe), this trombone is *My Fair Lady*.

I've grown accustomed to her case,
I've come to love her splotchy scales.
I've grown accustomed to her slide.
It doesn't always glide;
It's bruised, confused,
A bit abused.

But she's the horn I know so well
Up from the spit valve to the bell.

I know I threw her over for a horn from New Orleans.
While I played, she languished many years in
quarantines.

Oh but I love my 3-B King.
It's more than just a fling!
I've grown accustomed to her case.

Chapter 13

The Beat Goes On

Three years after I retired, I returned to Denver for my 50th high school reunion. Thomas Jefferson High, bordered by Happy Canyon Road, had morphed from a white suburban mecca to an integrated magnet school for technology. But not everything had changed since 1967. When Jeremy Stone and I slipped into the TJ choir room, he sat behind the same grand piano that had been there our senior year. Jeremy was a concert pianist, had become the youngest musical director of a Broadway show (*Grease*) in the 1970s and, after earning a Ph.D. in psychology, began counseling New York kids who had harmed or tried to kill themselves. But now, in the school's choir room, he was humoring an ex-classmate who had come up with 50th-reunion words to a familiar song. He quickly picked out the proper key and a flourishing intro that set me up for an evening performance.

Yesterday – Metamucil seemed so far away,
Colonoscopy was hard to say.
Oh, I believed in yesterday.

Suddenly, we're four times older than we used to be –
Medicare, Social Security.
Oh, yesterday went suddenly.

Why we had to age, I don't know, He would not say.
Youth is all the rage but – do we long for yesterday?

I didn't quit my day job because daily newspapers were being gutted. I didn't quit, I might add, to become a professional trombonist, either. I loved my newspaper job and the freedom that went with it. I loved the city that I first viewed as nothing more than a way station. Most of all, I treasured my long relationship with *Press-Enterprise* readers. I left in 2014, nearly sixty-five but still young enough to drive a car, because I feared being haunted by a question I'd never be able to answer: What if I had tried something else?

Gripped by a mild state of panic over all the unfilled time suddenly at my disposal, I probably tried too much. I hosted a jazz show for UC Riverside's radio station, updated a history of the *Press-Enterprise* for the local historical society, began to research a book about the paper's U.S. Supreme Court victories in the 1980s and hooked up with a young deputy district attorney who ran a program called Real Men Read. Each week, we visited locked-down units that housed juvenile offenders. Some of these kids had never read a book. But now they had plenty of time and we tried to help them fill it with almost anything they wanted, from *Harry Potter* to *Diary of a Wimpy Kid* to *Lord of the Flies.* (We denied periodic requests for a book that explained how to make a bomb.) When the pandemic shrank Real Men Read to a stay-at-home Zoomer, Candia and I hooked up with the local food bank and made weekly deliveries to people, including children, who were living on the edge. Others were shut-ins, had just lost their jobs or were simply afraid to go out.

Not everything was new in retirement. Candia and I continued to take our Old English sheepdogs to herding lessons, or as she called it, "sheep school," which we discovered in 2005. True to my sworn oath to *do anything for a column*, I drove to a sheep ranch in a rural community south of Riverside. When the herding trainer declared that Seymour had a "strong work ethic," it shocked everyone, including the dog. Though not at all like playing trombone in a brass quintet, Seymour and I aspired to achieve our own synchronized swing as we tried to steer moody, flighty or just plain stubborn sheep to a given destination. After Seymour passed on, his successors – Marvin, Sherman and Harry – were called upon to display *their* work ethics. Results varied.

Another holdover from the day-job days, of course, was my trombone. I was thrilled to be back in the RCC jazz ensemble. I also enrolled in a music theory class taught by a popular, highly respected professor – and my good friend. She was demanding, endlessly patient and committed to doing whatever she could to help students succeed. I dropped out anyway. I had a lot going on at the time – a new dog, a new book, plenty of good excuses. But I also felt overwhelmed. I just wasn't grasping theory as quickly as I'd hoped. It felt so much like *math!* When I dropped the course, I felt relief – and regret.

BrassWorks continued to replenish its ranks with splendid musicians who (except for me) were gainfully employed. But we became a performing group rather than a rehearsal group, gathering to work up sets when we got gigs instead of grinding through new music under the gentle gaze of a taskmaster. Those glory days were behind me. I also stuck with a gig I started before I retired: a one-man band, but not on a street corner and without a monkey. They call it music therapy. I started out at a Riverside hospital and later on hooked up with an assisted-living complex in Oregon.

The Lodge is located in the Central Oregon city of Sisters. That's where I met Joe Holder, the white-ponytailed gentleman you met in the prologue. Joe, at ninety, was still kicking himself for giving up his trumpet and flugelhorn when he got out of high school. I played for Joe and others once a week during summers, dipping into my library of play-along jazz and pop. One lovely woman always sat so close to me that I could have easily poked her with my slide. I was told she was virtually blind and very hard of hearing, but could feel the pulse and vibrations of the music.

This small audience of septuagenarians-and-up expanded my repertoire mainly because I didn't always play what they wanted to hear. After my unofficial girlfriend, Carol, pined for "You Are the Sunshine of My Love," I found a play-along book of Stevie Wonder hits. When another asked for "Dock of the Bay," I bought a book of soul tunes. When they continued to lob requests I could not fulfill, I put down my ax and became a YouTube DJ.

One afternoon, several residents asked for a song they first heard when they were kids:

Let's get it on!
Ah, baby, let's get it on!
Let's love, baby!
Let's get it on, sugar!
Let's get it on, woo hoo!

As they smiled and swayed from their wheelchairs or filled their lungs with auxiliary oxygen or tobacco, I scanned the YouTube comments posted beneath the video. "Statistically speaking," read one, "there is a good chance someone was born because of that concert…" It is also conceivable that some of these newborns were now sitting in The Lodge's sheltered courtyard, listening to Marvin Gaye's soulful plea to let's do you-know-what. When summer ended, I returned to Riverside and resumed music therapy at Kaiser Hospital. The pandemic shut me down (Caution: Lethal Trombone Droplets), but I will be back.

THE FEET ARE ALWAYS the tell. Once I start playing, I scan the room. If I see a foot keeping time, I settle in and settle down. I know the music is getting through to someone in the toughest room I've ever played: Kaiser's Oncology Unit, where patients receive their cancer-killing cocktails. Chemo.

Riverside is now 330,000-plus large. But small enough for me to have known some of these patients before they got sick. I've gotten to know others because I show up on the day of their regular infusions. Some request songs. Some even clap when the song ends. Others completely tune me out, moving their feet to the beat that arrives through their earbuds. Even without music therapy, this large room has a soundtrack: insistent electronic monitors that won't stop beeping until someone turns them off; nurses bustling from patient to patient; family members buzzing in conversation with nurses, loved ones or other visitors; patients, reclining in long, padded "infusion chairs" and talking about the music they love and the instruments they've played.

It's a different scene in the ICU. When Melissa Ortega, who worked in the intensive care unit, invited me up to play, I thought she was just being polite and let it pass. A trombone in ICU conjured images of that legendary *toro* ambling through a boutique stocked with only the finest Wedgewood. But when she asked again, I agreed without knowing exactly what I was agreeing to.

ICU is exactly what you think it is: The patients are very sick. But there is another condition that is so obvious that it never crossed my mind. The stress level of nurses, doctors and all the other personnel that comprise this life-or-death unit can veer sharply into the red zone. Music changes the mood. This is what I have been told. And what I have seen. I can't tell you what happens physiologically or mentally when the music starts, but as a trombone-wielding layman, I recognize dancing nurses when I see them. I'm familiar with group sing-alongs, especially Christmas carols. I've become acquainted with children and grandchildren, compliments of ICU folks' videos of their young piano players, drummers and guitar heroes. These mood-changing dances, songfests and shared video sessions do not last long. We're talking seconds, seldom more than a minute. Then the dancers and singers return to their real world while I keep playing. It's a privilege, an honor. And tremendously rewarding. It is exactly where I want to play my horn.

If I'm not in oncology or ICU, I'm in the well-trafficked public area where people buy their coffee and snacks and sit around tables waiting for prescriptions to be filled or appointments to start or maybe for a friend or relative who's undergoing a "procedure." I set up near the busy intersection of wide hallways. The acoustics are forgiving and the "audience" is mostly in motion. Some smile and give me the old thumbs up. Others walk or roll on by. Still others stop and listen, whipping out phones to take stills or videos. Though I'm not whistling or accompanying myself with an electric typewriter, live music in a hospital is still something of a novelty act. The trombone play-long to "Bohemian Rhapsody" is quite the head-turner.

I do not leave my case open, the international sign that tips are appreciated. I don't ask for them and I'm not supposed to. That is not why I'm there. When listeners quietly lay money on my music stand, I explain it will go to my favorite hospital charity: the unofficial dog-biscuit fund at the volunteer office. In addition to music therapy, Kaiser offers pet therapy. Candia has escorted two of our most affable sheepdogs, Marvin and Harry, through the hallways, waiting rooms and even hospital rooms of the labyrinthine hospital. These boys and other therapy canines have directly benefited from the occasional trombone tippers.

This part of the hospital, with its snack-bar vibe, is informal and chatty. Some kids have never seen a trombone, so I demonstrate its most unique feature: the slide's cartoonish *glissando* that can mimic the sound of a race car. I also have that toilet plunger that produces a forlorn *wah-wah-wah-wah*. Grown-ups stop to tell me their stories: the elderly gentleman who played his horn until he could no longer lift it; the proud mom whose daughter plays in a college jazz band; the grandfather who gave his grandson the guitar *he* used to play – turns out the kid is pretty good; the young trombone player who, unlike quite a few passersby, doesn't mistake my instrument for a trumpet.

I think of this public patch of Kaiser as a town square, a melting pot of the young and old, a broad palette of races, wardrobes, backgrounds and beliefs and medical histories. They stream to the square for any number of reasons, some routine, others worrisome, still others life-changing. Every so often, they stop to listen to music that transcends age, race, gender and social status as it unearths old stories – "My mother used to love that song," sighed a middle-aged woman after listening to "Stardust" – and creates new ones.

"God gave us twelve notes," said Jon Batiste on that Oscar night in 2021. "It's the same twelve notes that Duke Ellington had. Bach had." These notes – their infinite configurations and rhythms – sing to the "minds and hearts and souls" of every person who hears them, feels them. "Man, it's just so incredibly special."

Playing those notes in an ensemble, a hospital, even an isolated practice session that might give God second thoughts about handing out those twelve notes in the first place, *can* be an incredibly special feeling for every musician, even a fourth-grade thumb sucker who wound up with a trombone, lugged it into his seventies and managed to keep it out of the case even as he kept his day job.

Chapter 14

Nine to Five

Over three decades of column writing, I was always on the lookout for a sound or sight or even the slightest hint of music: a certain harmonica player, a symphony conductor, a music teacher, a fledgling non-profit that gave kids a chance to make music instead of trouble. These were stories about my community, stories I felt privileged to tell, loved to tell. The following columns are a lightly edited collection of music-related stories. I have also included two that sing to me in a very personal way: one about my father and one about my mother.

The Most Beautiful Ceremony Ever

HE STANDS ON a hill, framed by a canopy of small pines, waiting.

He is nervous. You wouldn't think he would be. He has done this countless times, including once, it seemed, in front of the whole world. But he's nervous.

"You just stand there and you wait until the end," he explained. "You're just standing there. You're watching these families. You know they'll remember for the rest of their lives. And some videotape it. Not only will they remember it, but they'll replay it."

Finally, the signal. Sometimes, it's a nod, sometimes a gesture. Sometimes, the crack of a rifle.

Keith Doxie, until now motionless and practically invisible in his dark blue, double-breasted Armani suit, raises his trumpet to his lips and the sad, final, consoling strains of "Taps" take flight from a hilltop at Riverside National Cemetery.

It is over in 20 seconds. Keith Doxie walks back to his car, having played his second, and last, military funeral of the day.

"I could do this full time," he marvels, mindful of the irony of his budding career. Former Airman Keith Doxie never liked playing funerals.

Doxie has lived in Moreno Valley since 1984 when he got his orders for March Air Force Base. He played in the band, of course. He played funerals, reluctantly. It just wasn't great duty. As he rose through the ranks, he savored the chance to order other airmen to play funerals.

But when he left the Air Force in 1992, Keith Doxie joined the ranks of struggling musicians. Now 31, he looks at military funerals in a different light.

He puts it this way: "I needed a gig."

He needed a gig. The 15th Air Force Band of the Golden West, a defense-budget casualty, is being deactivated. And the Riverside National Cemetery, second-busiest in the country, averages nearly 23 funerals a day. It sounded like a fit.

So several weeks ago, the industrious bugler spent four days poring over SoCal Yellow Pages, compiling a mailing list and sending letters to 250 mortuaries. The phone soon began to ring.

Keith Doxie, offering "Professional Bugle Details in accordance to military regulations & protocol" charges $65 per funeral. A pittance, he concedes, especially considering what a ceremony is like without him.

"Imagine an honor guard accompanying the casket. The honor guard with weapons on the hill. They have the service, say a prayer, give the final salute, shoot off the guns and present arms. That's when you pay 'Taps.'"

And if there's no one to play it?

"They play a tape. It's pretty disgusting. They have a little portable tape player. So, if you can imagine a tape after a ceremony . . ."

It is 15 minutes before a funeral. Doxie arrives at one of the cemetery's staging areas, where cars, vans, motorcycles and mourners gather for the procession to one of several cabana-like shelters.

His horn is only five years old, but looks 75. Old pennies, from the Eisenhower years, are shinier. The bell is cockeyed. He doesn't flash it around, but some clients – or their representatives – catch sight of his trumpet. "It worries 'em." It needn't.

Doxie would love to warm up, blow a few notes, maybe a few scales, something, anything to distract him. He's nervous. "The thing I love to do scares me the most."

He must have been petrified in 1986. After the Challenger exploded, Doxie and another airman were dispatched to the Crystal Cathedral to play "Taps" for a huge, televised memorial service. "It was definitely high pressure. I was very nervous. You just sit there and you wait until the end. If you bork the note, everybody knows."

He didn't bork the note, of course. He didn't bork any notes at the cemetery, either. He is a first-rate trumpeter and plays Latin jazz with Double Vision at Mario's Place. He even named his kid Miles.

But at the cemetery he played "Taps" strictly by the book – with a melancholic clarity, "in accordance to military regulations & protocol."

"I could play 'New York, New York' in Palm springs and be absolutely miserable," said Doxie. "Or, I could do this. When you see the ceremony, you'll understand. The military is so tradition-bound. It's the most beautiful ceremony ever."

Stan Kaye, Rock Star

August 5, 2012

On Christmas Eve 1944, Stan Kaye watched a burly coal miner put a nickel in a pay phone. When his mom answered, the Pennsylvania miner removed a box from his pocket, extracted something from it and, standing right there in the Kaye family's bar, played "Silent Night."

Eleven-year-old Stan was astounded. "You could carry music around in your pocket?" Christmas Day, he walked four miles and spent $2 on a harmonica.

Last Sunday, Stan Kaye walked onto the Municipal Auditorium stage and astounded the audience for "Riverside's Got Talent," a talent show/fundraiser sponsored by the Uptown Kiwanis Club. He was all nerves as the emcee introduced him. But when he began to "make love" to his favorite harmonica, Stan thought, "I'm home again." By night's end, the 79-year-old Moreno Valley resident was also $1,000 richer, top prize among adult contestants.

Recalling that Christmas Eve, Stan said, "Little hinges swing big doors." Just out of high school he played harmonica on national radio and TV. He played his harmonica in the Air Force and helped put himself through college, playing at nightclubs. "I once played with a 75-piece symphony backing me up. I had offers to go pro."

But he wanted to come to California to "make a difference with people." So began a career working with "young, tough, delinquent boys" in various county and state agencies. He worked in hospice and in prisons. He moved to Moreno Valley 21 years go. Before retiring in 2000, he contracted as a therapist with Riverside County's children's protective services. He "married late" and divorced. No kids.

Through all those years, Stan rarely played his harmonica. He tried a comeback, but "surgery and health issues thwarted that." Then, last November, he played a Veteran's Day gig at Riverside's Janet Goeske Center and the man who never took a music lesson "started to get back into it."

Next, he played in Goeske senior center's talent show and then heard about the Kiwanis contest. Dozens auditioned; 23 made the cut: singers, dancers, pianists, a juggler and more. Stan entered at the last minute, knowing he was headed for heart surgery, but not knowing when.

Last Sunday, Stan blew away the crowd with *"Malagueña,"* a classic Spanish piece that is both frenetic and pensive. "I had a three-minute slot. I wanted to show off what the harmonica could do, catch them by surprise." It must have worked. A digital applause meter, counting for half a contestant's score, soared into the 90s. It took time before Stan got excited about winning.

> It's not what I went down there for. I really wanted to
> play a good-sized room again, and I wanted exposure
> because I want to volunteer at veterans' hospitals.

But he was surprised and moved by the sincerity of the kids who said they never knew a harmonica was so versatile. He began to think, "I might could win a thousand bucks here."

Following next month's heart surgery, he'll plan "the next 80 years." Making love to his Hering Opus will be part of it. Stan Kaye is back and smiling.

"I'm an 80-year-old rock star!"

The Power of Tower

September 24, 1989

Anyone know a craftsman who specializes in bronzing trombones? Mine's ready for retirement. What more could I hope to achieve after spending an hour in Jazz 1, belting out "Witchcraft" with the Hemet High Jazz Band?

May I assume that you have heard of this band? You're alive, no? Vital signs normal? Then, surely you've heard the Hemet High Jazz Band on the radio. Or maybe you caught them at the Playboy Jazz Festival. This fall, they'll play in Chicago and Portland. Tomorrow, they'll play Riverside in that big glass house of county government. Then, they'll probably wash the windows. These kids love to work. That Jazz 1 class starts at 7:28 a.m.

I horned my way in into the band by asking director Jeff Tower if I could sit in on the early-morning class. He hadn't heard me play, so he said yes. I found my way to the band room, which could have been mistaken for the Hemet Plaque and Trophy Co. "Dan's a fine trombonist from Riverside," he told the band. I began to understand why this jazz program enjoys such a towering reputation. This guy could sell anything.

Jeff Tower has a deep, FM-radio voice and knows how to use it. He drives these kids. Not mean, but hard. Seven-thirty a.m. hard. Six-thirty a.m. when a concert draws near. He doesn't talk down to the band. He comes right at them.

He tells the bass player that there's no way she should be intimidated by a tricky solo. You've been hearing this chart for a couple of years, he says. You're not a kid anymore.

He advises a trombone player to write out a solo, not wing it. "Don't try to play by ear. Your ear's not good enough yet."

He complains about "stupid" mistakes and doesn't hesitate to identify the trumpet player who has missed a string of notes "every time you've played it."

He issues warnings about the risks of not practicing.

But when he discusses the upcoming trip to Chicago, he promises, "We'll knock 'em dead!"

Tower, 36, is in his 13th year at Hemet High. He views himself as a coach and he talks like one. "I don't think Hemet is any more talented than any other area. There's just more commitment on everybody's part to our program."

Everybody includes the kids, of course. They don't mind being pushed because he's trying to get them to play better.

Everybody includes school administrators who, unlike those in other districts, wouldn't think about laying off band directors.

Everybody includes parents – boosters – whose weekly bingo games finance band operations. And donors who help sustain a budget that approaches six figures. "Without community and financial help, we don't get outside of Hemet. We don't record albums."

Perhaps most important, "everybody" includes band directors from Hemet High's feeder schools – the middle and elementary school "farm teams."

If Hemet High has built a musical dynasty, Tower knows there's no guarantee it will last forever. "Teachers move on, administrators change, the community loses focus, instructors are not as talented or motivated."

But for now? "Our administration understands the concept, if it works, don't fix it."

They were kind to me in Jazz 1, politely ignoring my untimely splats. When the hour ended, everyone left. Another day, another rehearsal. No big deal, though it was for me.

I envied those musicians for their 7:28 a.m.s. Sometimes, the bell rings much too soon.

The ex-Kid From Hemet

A DOZEN YEARS ago, I invited myself to sit in on a rehearsal with Hemet High School's legendary jazz band.

Director Jeff Tower put me on second trombone, but the main thing he did was put me next to his lead 'bone player. The unspoken message: Just follow Jennifer and you'll be fine.

Jennifer Krupa graduated that spring and I lost track of her. But a few weeks ago, her mother called. She figured I might be interested in what had become of her daughter.

Jennifer received her BA in Florida and hung around the Hanging Chad State to play Dixieland. But a few years ago, she attended a conference in New York City and fell in love. With the Big Apple. She decided to move there because, to her mind, anyone who aspired to be a professional musician – a jazz trombonist – had no choice.

"I was attracted to jazz when I first listened to it," remembered the ex-kid from Hemet. "I like the freedom of expression. I like to interact with other musicians. I love to be able to create music."

Now she was in New York, renting an apartment and striking deals with her fellow tenants: No practicing after 10 p.m.

She practices two to three hours a day, not counting gigs. "I work on the fundamentals, making sure I can play the trombone." She doesn't complain that this drill can be frustrating, tedious and demanding. She may not even think of it that way. This is her passion. Only one person makes Jennifer play her ax: Jennifer.

> There's a sweetness to the trombone. There's a real
> raw side, too. I try to focus on playing soulful at all
> times. I want to be able to tell a story.

She tells this story: When she was in fourth grade, the owner of a Hemet music store informed her, "Girls don't play trombone." But by the time I first met her in 1989, Jennifer had been Hemet High's lead jazz trombone player for three years.

"For a girl to be leading a trombone section is an unusual case of affairs," her band director, Jeff Tower, explained at the time. "She's real aggressive, she has a good confidence level, her mom pushes her hard and being a woman trombonist in a world full of men, you always have something to prove."

Life after Hemet High has seen Jennifer prove herself time and again. She has played with the Benny Goodman Orchestra and performed with such jazz greats as trumpet wizard Clark Terry and Wycliffe Gordon, the trombonist she regards as her mentor.

And, yes, she has also played her share of clinkers: weddings and conventions – the can't-be-picky gigs that full-time musicians cannot afford to turn down. The worst? A Christmas party awash in synthesized music. Four horn players, including Jennifer, were ordered to make up parts that fit the synthesizer.

The best? Last summer, a trombone player with the Lincoln Center Jazz Orchestra fell ill and Jennifer filled in for the rest of the international tour, playing for orchestra leader Wynton Marsalis. Now 29, Jennifer has landed the gig of her young life: She was one of 18 jazz musicians admitted to the first class of the Julliard Institute for Jazz Studies, a two-year program she hopes will launch her on her dream: She wants to be a touring jazz musician.

She had to audition for this program. She sent in a tape, made the cut, then auditioned live. Now, she'll be learning from the masters, including Marsalis, who has taken a few media lumps for alleged sexism. Jennifer hasn't felt it.

> He's very nice to me, very encouraging. He tells me
> to make sure I keep developing my own sound, and
> that it doesn't matter if you're a woman or not.

Someone should have mentioned this to that Hemet music store owner before he counseled that little fourth-grader. But it really didn't matter. Jennifer Krupa knew better – and ignored him.

A Debut of Note

APRIL 25, 2008

Just a few months ago, Heather Hodges was in tears as she pleaded with Val Verde school boarders to spare the elementary music program from budgetcide.

Now, here she was, seated in front of a small stage with a flute in her lap. I hadn't met Heather yet. Had no idea who she was. I just saw a tiny white-haired lady with a flute and hoped someone would be able to hear her. Because I also saw two or three drum sets. A Stonehenge of amps. A set of congas. Upright electric basses. Electric guitar and keyboard. A trio of trumpet players, a couple of saxes and a lone trombone (mine). At least Heather had company – another flutist.

Six months from now, the Riverside Jazz and Arts Exchange might be a household name. Co-founders Jim Palmer and Joe McNally got their feet in the door of a 7,000-square-foot building. Now the trick is to fill it with kids, paid teachers, musicians, dancers. It's a non-profit, booze-free biz plan, heavily dependent on grants, good will and trust. But those chapters are yet to be written. This was Day One – The Unveiling. An old-fashioned come one, come all Sunday afternoon jam session.

Here's how these things work: Someone picks a tune. "Blue Bossa." "Black Orpheus." "Green Dolphin Street." "Yellow Submarine." Then everybody plays, or fakes, the melody once or twice. Then anyone who wants to solo, which means make something up, gets a moment in the sun (or a scalding on the hot seat).

When it was Heather's turn, Jim Palmer positioned a mike near her flute just so and I craned my neck, hoping to catch a faint note or two. It didn't take long before I stopped craning. Heather Hodges (Ramona High School Class of '65) plays a crisp, hard-driving jazz flute. The woman can swing.

Her dad was a band director at Ramona. Her daughter is the band director at Riverside's University Heights Middle School. Her son-in-law helped lead the successful campaign to save elementary music in Riverside. Heather teaches at two Val Verde elementary schools – from kindergarten up – and gives private lessons. But she came to this unveiling for an uncomplicated reason.

"I needed to play." Not teach. Just play.

> It's very cathartic for me. When I discovered jazz, improvising in general, there's so much freedom to that. It feels so good. It's of the moment. You just toss it out there.

It's about ideas. Thinking of them. Executing them. In the moment. Much like what Jim Palmer and Joe McNally are trying to do with their jazz and art exchange.

"I was very impressed with the place," said Heather. Not just the jam session, but with the sprawling downtown building west of Market on Sixth Street. "It has potential as a place to teach and as a place for kids. I would love to continue what I do with early childhood stuff."

This is what Palmer and McNally would like to offer, at a low price. But it will take good, tough chops and lots ingenuity to make it real.

Let the improvisation begin.

Riverside School of the Arts

December 15, 2013

THE STORIES RESONATE even louder than the music:

The autistic pianist who performs at the school fundraiser while his mom guards a trash can. Nearly homeless, she isn't about to leave without the bottles and cans.

Leslie Carillo, 13, who had wanted to learn guitar since, well, forever, strums a Christmas carol in a small class taught by a volunteer. "She's learning something instead of walking the streets with her friends," said her mom, Maria. Learning on a school guitar.

Margarita Herrera brings her 9-year-old grandson, Isaiah, to this school three days a week for drum and guitar lessons. "I'm trying to find ways to keep his mind busy. It teaches him to concentrate in school, gives him something for the future."

These stories resonate even louder when you learn there are up to 275 of them (there were more than 500 last summer). And to think that the Riverside School of the Arts, located in the Cesar Chavez Community Center on the Eastside, is barely a year old.

It is a school for anyone, but not for everyone. Councilman Andy Melendrez represents the Eastside and helped launch the school. "We're serving individuals who aren't able to pay $30 per hour or half hour for lessons."

For now, it is a labor of love, nourished by local businesses, non-profits, volunteer instructors and steely parents and grandparents determined to keep kids in line and give them a chance. Donated time. Donated instruments. The kind of sacrifice a start-up needs to survive. But how long can it survive?

From 3:30 till 7:30 each weekday afternoon, students learn to tackle the basics of ballet or violin. Learn from whom? California Riverside Ballet. Musicians and artists. There's even an orchestra. How much does it cost the kids? Virtually nothing.

This is the magic and the mission of the school of the arts. In the eyes of its strongest backers, including Melendrez, Parks & Rec chief

Ralph Nunez and Collette Lee, a Riverside realtor, the school is proving its worth. This is code for: it deserves a home in the city budget.

It almost didn't get this far. Amid rumors it was going under (it was never in the budget but Nunez found ways to staff it here and there), biz and non-profits and even electeds (county supervisors with slush funds!) rushed to the rescue.

Nunez said about $38,000, including a good chunk from Riverside's recent Give Big campaign, has been raised or promised. Councilman Steve Adams donated a drum set. Ex-Councilman Ken Gutierrez donated his dad's trumpet.

Collette Lee, a fundraising ring leader: "I wish they (the city council) would donate the funding."

Now, there's an idea with a beat kids could dance to!

UPDATE: Thanks to its dogged fundraising, the renamed Riverside Arts Academy has survived and continues to receive annual grants from the California Arts Council. In 2021, it scored its largest haul yet: $30,000. The Riverside Jazz and Arts Exchange, alas, did not make it.

His Legacy is His Encore

SEPTEMBER 16, 2008

YEARS AGO, I stood backstage at Riverside's Municipal Auditorium, chatting with the general manager of the Riverside County Philharmonic. It was almost 8 p.m. on a Saturday. The concert would start any minute. Everything was in its place. Except Patrick Flynn. The conductor hadn't arrived and the GM was quietly losing his mind. He looked at his watch. Then the door. Watch. Door. Door. Watch. No Flynn.

The differential between Flynn and Pacific standard times had evidently become such a sore point that a punctuality clause had been inserted into the maestro's contract. Yet, here it was, just seconds till showtime and – and there he was! Breezing through the very doorway the GM had placed under surveillance. The lanky Flynn didn't look rushed or harried. He looked cool and ready to go to work. He hardly broke stride as he dispensed hellos and strode on stage to hearty applause.

Patrick Flynn, who died last week, could be exasperating. Maybe he intended to be. But he was worth it. I don't know if he was a genius, but he nailed the ultimate test: He made the orchestra better than it was when he arrived 20 years ago.

One of the first musicians Flynn hired played flute and piccolo. Karen Togashi lives in Orange County and plays in other orchestras besides the RivCo Phil. What was it like playing for Patrick Flynn?

"He really had extraordinary ears. He heard everything." And he was a risk taker. "You always went in knowing something was going to be different or unusual or you were going to have your mindset challenged."

Often, said Togashi, it worked. "You'd think, 'Wow! I wonder why no one's done that before!'"

Other times, she'd think: "Wow! That's why no one's done that before!"

Flynn could be difficult. Scathing. I couldn't imagine the guy voluntarily staging children's concerts. I figured some higher-up had forced him into it. But I soon saw how much he loved talking to kids about music and instruments and bringing them on stage to conduct. He enjoyed it so much that the cash-strapped orchestra sometimes doled out overtime pay to 70 musicians.

Togashi and I recalled our spontaneous "escapade" during one of these children's concerts. Karen played her piccolo and then I whistled as we split that famous solo in "Stars and Stripes Forever."

Togashi said Flynn liked surprises. "Because he was unconventional, he had a respect for unconventional things. Any other conductor would have fired me on the spot. He thought it was a riot."

I asked Karen what Patrick Flynn left behind.

> From a musician's standpoint, if you have a different
> idea musically and you're passionate about it and
> you commit to it, you can make it work and it can be
> a truly new, refreshing, exciting experience for the
> performer and the listener alike. He wasn't one to
> muddle along with the *status quo*.

As Riverside and the inland region grew, Togashi said the orchestra started "along the path from being a disorganized provincial ensemble to a more professionally minded group. I think he had something to do with it. He was charismatic with the patrons and the donors."

And if a GM sweated bullets before a concert, that was part of the package. A maestro who muddled along with the *status quo* would have put the GM (and the audience) sound to sleep.

The Night the Band Played On

If they ever make another movie about a band director, I could suggest a scene. And it actually happened Tuesday when Jerry Lees conducted the Corona Community Concert Band.

The Corona Civic Auditorium is a beautiful Spanish-style building with an exposed-beam ceiling and huge, heavy chandeliers. It's warm and intimate, with only 383 seats. The civic auditorium is a fine place for a concert.

But when Maestro Lees brought down his baton for the opening number, John Philip Sousa's arrangement of "The Star-Spangled Banner," the audience consisted of 15 people. Conductors are supposed to play to packed halls. They're supposed to bask in the "Bravos!" This conductor gazed out at a sea of Corona empties. My heart went out to him.

It's not easy to put on a community band concert. There are hours of night rehearsals. Some musicians show up. Some don't. The conductor is always there. Band members certainly don't get paid and whatever conductors make won't make them rich and famous. Which is why you don't see many movies about them.

But Jerry Lees proceeded as if the Corona Community Concert Band had been booked into Carnegie, even though the program itself seemed to snicker at the sparse "crowd." One piece was called, "Where No Man Has Gone Before." But Lees coaxed the band to give the best concert it possibly could. When a selection concluded, the audience clapped and Lees, looking sharp in his black tuxedo, descended the conductor's stand and took a crisp, appreciative bow. He knew there were only 15 people out there. He even managed to smile about it. It was a scene that could come right out of a movie. Someday, maybe it will.

All Hail the Band of Dropouts

January 28, 1990

A brassy fanfare, please, for Amy Smith, Matt Greer and Jana Perry. They've dropped out of the Norco High School band.

Amy, frustrated clarinetist, is actually transferring to dreaded rival Corona High. Matt, a trumpet player, already made the move. Jana, also of the clarinet persuasion, will stay at Norco. But she'll drop band. Others may do the same.

Harold Hill, where are you?

Refreshing, in these times where study after study tells us how stupid kids are, to hear about a few who know what they want, know what they're not getting and do something about it. Amy, Matt and Jana don't like the Norco band because it doesn't sound like much of a band. The music's too easy. The band has no money. The director won't ask for any. And he won't let anyone else, like parents, raise it.

The kids? They're tired of wasting their time.

The band director disagrees with these reviews, vigorously rebutting every charge. Fine. But the defections speak for themselves.

And Norco ain't alone.

In California, between 1982 and 1986, the number of students playing in high school bands and orchestras was cut in half – from 125,000 to 65,000. This from a recent music-in-the-schools piece in the *LA Times*.

Why? Shriveled budgets, for one. And a suspicion that music education is an air-headed frill. Take it from Amy, Matt and Jana: It's not. And take it from me – a guy who, in those critical early years, learned to carry a tune *and* carry the 1. I have no trouble telling you which exercise I now find more satisfying.

High school bands don't have to go sour. Hemet's hasn't. Corona's hasn't. Corona band members get cheers. Norco band members get applause. "It's rejoicing because we're finished," lamented poor Amy Smith. No wonder she decided to switch schools.

There's a clear message here, and the kids – brain dead as those studies say they are – are sending it. They want better. They *demand* better. They're entitled to better. And the schools *had* better.

Didja Know There's a Band of Didgeridoos?

October 20, 2013

THE BAND MEMBERS sitting in a circle cup their hands over their ears, the better to hear themselves blow, or drone, into the instruments gripped between their knees.

The sound is unlike anything produced by any middle school band anywhere. Members of the Indigenous Tribes band at Riverside's Wells Middle School are playing didgeridoos.

These are long, tubular instruments crafted from agave, yucca, pepper, cedar, oak, you name it. This instrument literally traces its roots back thousands of years to the Aboriginal tribes of Australia. It produces a deep-to-the-core, vibrating sound, punctuated by invented rhythms and tempo changes as the didgeridoo player becomes more proficient.

Talk to teachers and the principal and you soon learn Wells Middle is one of the poorest in the area. More than 80 percent of the students receive subsidized lunches. But some are extraordinarily well off thanks to Myke Gomezmaicas ("Mr. G") and Geoff Tucker, who, in addition to their other duties as educators, have been teaching "didges" and drums in the Indigenous Tribes band for nine years.

Mr. G, 37, who describes himself as "half white, half Cuban" is the didge man. He spotted a connection between the bleak messages in the hip-hop music he loves and the Aborigines, who were shunned for playing "the Devil's music." He took up the didge and now makes them. Without Mr. G's craftsmanship (the band started with plastic pipe from Home Depot), Wells kids would have didgerisquat.

Geoff Tucker, 24, teaches drums. He is a natural communicator who seems to effortlessly reach his students. But none of this begins to describe what Mr. T and Mr. G have done for a decade.

"At the first of the year, we're like drill sergeants," says the tall and tattooed Mr. G. "We tell the kids that some of them won't be around in a couple of weeks."

They might be giving away lessons (the kids pay $5 for drum sticks; that's about it), but Mr. G and Geoff Tucker are selling something too:

the importance of discipline, dedication and, yes, the dreaded P-word: practicing.

Unlike whistling, you don't just put your lips together and blow. Didgeridoo players must learn to play while they exhale *and* inhale. Circular breathing is so hard to learn that when a student finally gets it, Mr. G makes them a didgeridoo.

Jose Guillen, a sixth-grader, joined the band "after my sister told me it was great." He learned circular breathing "just like that." Sixth-grader Melissa Marin signed up because "I saw my cousin play. I thought it was awesome."

So awesome that Notre Vista high school kids come back to Wells for the weekly practices and help teach the little kids how to play and listen to each other. This band gives the kids a sense of belonging and confidence and diverts them from after-school life on the streets. Principal David Ferguson puts it simply: "It saves them."

Music teacher Myke Gomezmaicas demonstrating the didgeridoo
for students at Riverside's Wells Middle School, 2013.

That Old Trombone Magic

NOVEMBER 9, 1997

I'm SITTING IN a big room with a bunch of trombone players – a phenomenal bunch, as it turns out. Ordinarily, there are eleven of them. Today, there are just eight, but even this is a staggering number. We're playing at Riverside's Highland Elementary School because this is where everyone (except me) is supposed to be at 1 p.m.

They say Vegas has a book on everything. If you think the Dodgers will score more runs in the third inning than any other team next season, you can place the bet. But who would dare wager that an elementary school would have eleven trombones in a single class? Eleven trumpets? The world is crawling with them. Clarinets? They're a breeding ground for saxophones. But double-digit trombones? Julie Olson, Highland's music instructor, thought I should see this for myself.

Olson had finished cheerfully putting us through our paces: playing long notes, counting rests and sitting up straight. We began to talk about why we played this instrument. One little girl said she enjoyed finding notes with the slide and making her lips buzz. One boy hoped lugging his trombone around in its heavy case would develop his muscles. Another said he'd heard playing trombone helps improve handwriting. (I have disproved this theory.)

When it was my turn, I tried to say all the right things. It's a beautiful instrument. It's versatile. But I didn't tell them about Viola Austin.

I MET HER at summer music camp at the University of Colorado when we were high school sophomores. I'm not sure how I fell for a clarinet player, but I remember sitting in the audience and watching her band rehearse. I would look at her and she would sneak looks at me. You know how powerful The Look can be. We were smitten. And the fact that we lived in different states and would have to carry on a long-distance romance only heightened our divine state of smittenness.

Viola lived in McCook, Nebraska. I lived in Denver. We wrote letters, refusing to let a few hundred miles stand in the way of what was meant to be. Then, one day, she announced that she and her mom would visit Denver. For days, I could think of nothing else. Viola and I would go to dinner. We'd go to a movie. We'd talk about us.

Well before I ever met Viola, my dad tried to caution me about the hazards of resuming interrupted friendships, let alone summer romances. People change, he said. Don't get your hopes up. What did he know?

We went to dinner. We saw a movie. Whenever a post or a pole came between us as we walked downtown, Viola said, "Bread and butter." I had no idea what it meant, but I was sure she didn't say that to other guys. We had a nice time, but things had changed. Even though Viola said, "Bread and butter," she didn't give me The Look. After we said good night, our romance kind of fizzled.

Then, two weeks ago, I received a call. Viola was in Riverside, visiting her youngest daughter, a student teacher at Sherman Indian High School. Viola, now a Kansan, had subscribed to the paper to learn more about Riverside. She thought I looked familiar and decided to call. Viola made it a point to tell me that she was married and that her oldest daughter had come with her to Riverside. The three of us met for lunch.

As her twenty-seven-year-old daughter listened, Viola and I reminisced about music camp and our brief romance. When I reminded her that on the last night of camp we kissed in the parking lot, Viola's daughter cringed in apparent horror. She rolled her eyes and said, "I don't have to hear this." I had run my fingernails down the chalkboard of her life.

This is what I hadn't told my fellow trombonists at Highland Elementary: If I hadn't played trombone, I wouldn't have gone to music camp. I wouldn't have met Viola Austin. And I never would have been able to thoroughly embarrass her oldest daughter by recalling a parking-lot kiss between two 16-year-olds, one of whom would someday become her mother.

It was an unforgettable moment. I owe it all to my trombone.

Ramona High Students Give Guest a Piano Lesson

The second I walked in I knew I was in the right place. The Riverside classroom was packed with black upright pianos sitting side by side, row by row. Just like desks.

In a way, they *were* desks. The Ramona High School students stationed behind them variously hunted and pecked or played gracefully, fluidly.

Glancing up at the stranger, the students sensed my unease and pointed in the direction of the teacher. Ronda Barnes, as tiny as she is ageless, used to play French horn in a brass group that included me and my trombone. Ramona is a creative-and-performing-arts magnet school and Ronda is the "magnet coordinator." She also teaches piano classes with 150 students. Last week – Jazz Week – her students were learning the blues and Ronda invited me to attend.

Ronda thought improvised trombone playing or whistling would show how the scales provided a rich foundation – and inspiration. As the students played, I made up "music" to harmonize. The piano players artfully masked their winces when the notes escaping from my horn had no connection to the notes they were playing. (It was Jazz Week, I rationalized later, not Good Jazz Week.)

I don't know if the students learned much from me, but they gave me a refresher course in the magic of music.

There are about as many reasons as there are students for taking a piano class. Some do it to get their performing arts credit. Others are already in the band. Learning piano adds another dimension.

But some struggle with this 88-key monster, and who hasn't been tempted to quit when something got too tough? Some probably do, but not David Fierros, whom Ronda praised for plugging away, not giving up.

"Why not?" he smiled (and it was a big smile). "It sounds amazing."

Katelyn Kenzy is a senior who wants to be a doctor. She's headed to college and will study biology. But she's been playing piano for a good while and, with a little encouragement from the teacher, dusted off a piece she hasn't played that much lately. I can't even think fast enough to hum "Bumblebee Boogie," but there she was, probing the honeycomb of her memory as her fingers buzzed the keys.

It wasn't perfect, but it was there and once she played it, Katelyn yearned to "get my bumblebee back."

Once you make music, it's very hard to stop, and there are so many reasons not to.

"It keeps me grounded," said senior Jordan Westbrook, "so I won't do crazy things."

Music "empowers me," said sophomore Evan Kelly. The piano? "It has all the notes. You can play music on piano that on other instruments would be impossible." And there's this: "It's my escape. When there's an emotional build-up, playing piano relieves the pressure of everyday life."

Just a sophomore and he already knows this? Music is not just powerful and magical. It's portable. Even if you can't afford a piano – or a piano mover – it's always there, in your head (your feet, too) waiting to come out.

A student asked when I started playing trombone. Fourth grade, I answered. And here I was decades later, more than a little bald, more than a little gray, cracking notes, honking away. I hope the message got through: When it comes to music, you *can* take it with you.

Hear the One About the Racist Mascot?

OCTOBER 17, 1997

I HAD DECIDED not to write about the Stanford Band because I once was a member of this highbrow ensemble and am much too young to burden patient readers with brittle war stories. But in the last two weeks, I have received so many "your-band-really-did-it-this-time" looks. And the looks suggest that a once-scraggly trombone player who graduated during the Nixon administration is fully responsible.

What did the band do when Stanford hosted and defeated Notre Dame in a football game? From our wire services: During the halftime show, the band narrator called the Irish "stinking skunks" (the band disputes this). A parody of the Irish potato famine featured "Seamus O'Hungry," whose "sparse cultural heritage consisted only of fighting, then starving."

There was more, but you get the drift. According to news reports, Irish and Catholics in the stands were furious. The Catholic Diocese of San Jose demanded an apology. A newspaper editorial nailed band members for not even knowing what the potato famine was.

The Stanford Athletic Department apologized and denounced the show. The band has been banned, as I understand it, from Notre Dame games, home or away, for years to come. The band manager said people overreacted, the show was "misconstrued" and "taken out of context." The band's web page instructed: "For the Band's perspective on the recent Notre Dame slow-news-day frenzy, click here."

Slow-news-day frenzy? I checked to make sure I hadn't reached the Nixon (or Clinton) home page. Then I clicked to the "band's perspective." There were concessions: "We offended a group of people we had no intention of insulting." And, "We do take responsibility for the ambiguity of the script." And, "we apologize" – for the ambiguity.

But the "explanations" were jewels:

> *The concept behind the halftime show was not to insult*
> *Irish people, but to ridicule Notre Dame's racist mascot.*
> *We think it is absurd that Notre Dame can claim a*

*whole ethnicity as its mascot, and further characterize
this ethnicity as belligerent: the Fighting Irish. Further,
to represent the Irish, Notre Dame uses a leprechaun.
Most Irish people we know are not, in fact, leprechauns.*

Now do you understand why the show was funny?

I sit here, old and bald and ready to bite my tongue before I say, "Now
when I was in the band …" I can't say I'm proud of everything we did.
I can't even say I remember everything we did. But it's hard to forget
that at a place like Stanford, 'elitist" and "student" are often joined at
the hip. Band members would have been better off attending a seminar
on the potato famine before planning their halftime entertainment.

Or, failing that, simply admitting, "We're sorry. Our show really
sucked."

The Rhyme and Reason of Mel Tormé

NOVEMBER 15, 1994

A PORTRAIT OF my idol: He's got sad, bloodhound eyes and a rubbery face that balloons into a smile or deflates into an irritated frown. He's got a paunch just beneath his chin. He has thinning white hair and a fear of flying in clouds. He was born during the Coolidge administration but doesn't look nearly as wasted as Mick Jagger.

Tormé blew into Riverside – actually, he drove in from Phoenix rather than fly into thickening clouds – and performed for a brief hour in the Mission Inn Music Room. A weekend fundraiser for the Parkview Community Hospital Foundation. He sang his wonderful *Guys & Dolls* medley and his famously lucrative "Chestnuts roasting on an open fire ..." which he composed on a stiflingly summer day. He sang, scatted and even crooned to a packed and polished audience that, by apparent coincidence, happened to include a couple of his friends: Mel Brooks and his wife, Anne Bancroft.

I managed to weasel a pre-concert interview with Mr. Tormé, a gentleman I couldn't even stand until the late 1970s. That was when my patient pal, Gregg Sieja, sat me down in his wall-of-vinyl music room and instructed: "Listen to this!" And, "Now listen to this." And on and on. I felt like a music moron held hostage.

And now, here we were, just Mel and me, sitting in his rather opulent Mission Inn suite ("You wouldn't believe there'd be such a place in Riverside!" he marveled), discussing our mutual admiration for grunge rock. Well, not quite.

We sat in the Mission Inn and talked, fittingly, about master craftsmen. In this case, songwriters. Perhaps too modestly, Mel Tormé suggests it is the songwriters who hold the key to his lilting and acrobatic appeal.

"When young people get into their late teens and twenties," he observed, "they look for something more challenging than rock and roll. Rock and roll is three chords on a guitar. I'm not knocking it, but ..."

But Mel Tormé, who's 69 and sizzles in the same circles as Ella Fitzgerald, offers something different. Something, he says, more complex.

They're not new songs. They're old songs. Written by master craftsmen. People who did nothing but write songs. They wrote them and we grabbed them. Young people today sing and write their own songs. They're puerile lyrics. But they become hits, so who am I to say?

He's not knocking 'em.

They're not dark. They're mindless. Their lyric is like fast food. It comes and goes. But I'm not putting them down.

Of course not.

I just can't understand how they appeal to young people. But I'm not a young people.

He's an old pro with no one coming up to replace him – or Ella. No one, he says, in sight. Not that he's quitting, though he might rest up after 38 gigs in 36 cities.

He is a discriminating artist who picks his songs with care. "I like playlets. It has to tell a story. It has to be descriptive. It has to paint a picture."

And it will rhyme. Exquisitely. He loves the master-crafted internal rhyme.

Tormé tells the story of Zeelyox, a Buffalo optometrist who begged him to look at his song. Tormé finally gave in and the sample couplet went something like this:

You'll never know how much I love you sweetheart.
My love for you will last from dusk until dark.

Tormé informed the optometrist that "heart" and "dark" would never, ever rhyme.

What does Tormé want, you ask? What will satisfy this man? He recites his favorites without missing a beat:

While you love your lover let
Blue skies be your coverlet.

And:

That wonderful man Coolidge he
Delivered quite a eulogy.

But that evening, during his Music Room performance, something didn't sound quite Tormé-ish.

"You say you'll love me," he crooned, "and then you snub me."

"Love" and "snub"? A truly awkward Zeelyox moment.

Well, that's showbiz.

Mel Tormé and Dan Bernstein, 1994.

Letters From Home on Father's Day

JUNE 16, 1991

WHEN FATHER'S DAY arrives and a middle-aged man doesn't have a father anymore, not to mention a kid who might buy him a tie, there's a sense that this national holiday isn't quite for everyone, blockbuster Father's Day specials notwithstanding.

Unless, of course, the middle-aged man happens to be a pack rat.

I am that man.

A few days ago, I sat at home on a cloudy morning savoring a pack rat's bounty – letters from my dad, who died in 1985. They're more than a decade old. I received them when I was around 30. A grown-up. But still a subject of parental concern. Once a parent, I'm told, always, always, always so.

In one letter, my dad confesses to feeling guilty and stymied, having failed to come up with a present for our seventh wedding anniversary.

> *I think that the pleasure of the giver is much greater than that of the receiver. But what to give? I walked all through the third floor of the May D&F. I thought maybe a microwave oven, or perhaps serving platters, or silverware or glassware. But I couldn't make up my mind. I even talked to a Lady Clerk and she told me that the 7th anniversary is honored in copper and wooden articles. She had some antique kettles which made me think of a junkyard. I wandered through the store and nothing that we would have given would have given the pleasure I would like to feel. So, I am reduced to what we always do ... and we hope that you sincerely enjoy what you buy.*

Another letter, much longer, was prompted by an enclosure. My dad had just made the final payment on my $825 National Defense Student Loan. He sent me the receipt. This loan had helped me get through my freshman year at Colorado College in Colorado Springs. I had a good year there, but a restless one. I felt like The Only Kid Who

Had Never Left Colorado. The next year, I headed to California. Much to my father's dismay.

> *I shall always remember vividly that August day when you stood before us, buoyant and cheerful, holding a letter from Stanford in one hand. You almost shouted with exultation, elated that you were admitted to that great school. What could I say? Your joy did not pass from you to me. I, unlike you, felt somewhat dismayed. I visualized the difficulties of beginning anew in a new environment. You had proved yourself at CC. You were now a sophomore. You knew your way around. We flattered ourselves that being close would make it a little easier for you. But when I looked at your happy smile, I suppressed all my doubts. I hope I sounded enthusiastic when I spoke.*
>
> *When September came and you left for Palo Alto, I watched anxiously for word from you. I agonized over the distance you had to travel to school. Your lack of money. All the hardships which you endured, real or imagined. How often we wished for a weekend of the former year when we could see you; but parents' fears are often not justified.*
>
> *So I am happy to send you a reminder of a delightful year, one which I always remember with a sort of rejoicing and humility. I rejoice because of the happiness we felt because of your nearness for your first year in school. I am humble and grateful because my fears for your welfare were unfounded.*

My dad, I suspect, was no different from so many others. He loved his kids, yearned for us to be happy, worried about us, bit his tongue and worried some more. My dad learned that his kids were doomed to grow up, make mistakes, endure consequences. But we learned something, too: Our dad, Harry, was no Houdini. He couldn't escape being a parent. He worried about one or the other of us until the day he died. This is such a fundamental ingredient of parenthood that it is sometimes easy to forget – until you pick up a newspaper or turn on the TV and get bellyful of the horrible things that "newsmaker" parents to do their children.

My dad, I'm proud to say, never made the news.

Fragile yes, Timid no

Life, said the rabbi, "is fragile."

He could have been talking about Brian Cutter, the 19-year-old Riverside Marine who had been in Iraq two days when he was electrocuted fixing an air conditioner.

Or he could have been talking about Aryanna Sanchez, the 20-month-old toddler who drowned in a spa at a Riverside day-care center.

But as he spoke last Sunday, standing near a simple casket at a Denver cemetery, the eloquent rabbi – an old family friend – was talking about my 80-year-old mother.

I am relieved and grateful that her years of post-stroke suffering are over. But I already miss her. My older sister called her a "presence." More than that, she was our mother and no matter how we try to rationalize it – she lived a long life, she's free of pain, she's in a "better place" – Belle Bernstein is no longer a plane flight, phone call or even a cornball song away.

The family – four children and Gene, my mother's loving and thoroughly devoted companion – spent a long weekend in my mom's house, leafing through photo albums that added perspective to these last agonizing years. The photos served as a time machine, whisking us back decades, reminding us that our mother with the dazzling smile did not live her fragile life timidly.

She raised four children, racked up a trio of degrees, including a doctorate, became a head hunter, specializing in oil and gas. She shopped the globe, immersed herself in opera and had at least two good men fall head-over-heels in love with her.

Life is fragile, yes. But living doesn't have to be. Poor Aryanna Sanchez, the day-care baby, never got a chance to seize what life might have offered her. Brian Cutter couldn't wait to join the Marines. This was his dream and he didn't let it slip away.

Well before I was born, my mom had become somewhat notorious for asking, "What can happen?"

She knew what she wanted, knew how to get it and when all else failed, demanded to speak to the manager. She could be embarrassing, maddening and inspiring at the same moment.

Life will be different now. Different for Gene, who, at a vibrant 80, begins a new chapter in his life. Different for "the kids" no longer linked together by a parent.

A friend whose mother died several years ago told me not a day will pass when I don't think about my mom. Just now, I'm thinking too much about how she died early May 13, heavily drugged, refusing to take nourishment, alone.

In time, I expect to dwell more on how she lived. Even during the last three years, she could surprise me with her knowing giggle (usually following a joke about her awful cooking) or her knack for remembering lyrics.

When I sang, *"For it's root, root, root for the ..."* you could take it to the bank that she'd belt out, *"Yankees!"* The best mothers are always there for their children.

Which is why even the happiest memories can never replace the actual presence of the person who, whatever else she said or did, *always* answered to "mom."

Belle and Harry Bernstein on the day Belle received her PhD in Speech Communication from the University of Denver in 1974.
PHOTO BY DAN BERNSTEIN.

Endnotes

1. © 1973 Billy Joel.

2. Bernstein family papers.

3. *See* Tonette, *Wikipedia, https://en.wikipedia.org/wiki/Tonette*

4. Will Kimball, "Trombone History 15th Century," *https:// kimballtrombone.com/trombone-history-timeline/trombone-history-15th-century/*

5. "Navy Music Makers Hit the High Seas," *All Hands*, No. 631, August 1969: 14–15.

6. Daniel R. Cloutier, "Ludwig Van Beethoven's Orchestration of the Trombone," DMA dissertation, West Virginia University, 2009.

7. Dr. Kimberly Sena Moore, "The Subtle Impact of 'Pomp and Circumstance,'" *psychologytoday.com*, May 12, 2017.

8. Theresa Johnson, "The Greatest Hits of Arthur P. Barnes," *Stanford Magazine*, March/April 1997.

9. Hannah Knowles, "Fraught Mascot," *Stanford Daily,* September 20, 2018.

Acknowledgments

In the afterglow of a terrific concert or, for that matter, any other notable triumph, Charlie Richard's unfailing response to praise is, "It was a team effort." Whether this book merits any praise at all is not for me to say, but it was undeniably a team effort.

Charlie Richard and Chaz Warren were beyond generous with their time and support. So, too, were Danny Balancio, Jennifer Hall and Lisa Forster. Each gave me and, I hope, readers a much deeper understanding than I alone could have revealed about the challenges, hard work, satisfaction and pure joy of making music.

My sisters, Paula Remmel and Debra Green, my brother, Jeremy Bernstein and my cousin, Paul Stein, were indispensable sources, especially when it came to filling in the vast gaps in my knowledge of our family history.

I can't thank Jane Carney, Laurie Lucas and Russ Thompson enough. They took on the hapless task of being the first readers of the first draft. Their labor and their honesty helped me a great deal. Thank you to Larry Gulberg, the charismatic collegiate bass drummer, for taking the time to read the chapter about the Stanford Band.

I am grateful to Alex Henderson and Mark Prather for their love stories about their collections of trombones and trumpets. Huge thank yous to Carrie Rosema for the cover photo replicating the pose of an adolescent trombonist and to Ross Duffin, who was inspired to colorize the photo of that adolescent (and all that hair) on the back cover. Thank you to Jeannie Gayle Pool for her astute insights into marketing; and to Philip Neuman for his whimsical and witty illustrations. I am indebted to Jasminka Knecht, pianist, music professor and longtime friend who believed in this project from the start and encouraged me to keep at it during the inevitable periods of self-doubt.

Beverly Simmons and I met when we were teenagers at Temple Emanuel in Denver. We met again in college and then lost contact for many years after that. When we finally (and recently) reconnected, I discovered that her many talents – make that passions – included book design. From cover to cover, from font to photo to endnote, Bev designed the book you are holding in your hands. I am in awe of what she has produced.

Back in the early 1980s, when I started writing my newspaper column, my wife, Candia, had a much better grasp of what a column should be than I did. History repeated itself when I set out to write this memoir. Her insights and ideas about what was there, what was expendable and what was missing were as illuminating as they were indispensable.

I hate to imagine what would have finally landed between the covers of this book if the paperback writer had been a one-man band. I am grateful and honored to have been part of this challenging, joyful and thoroughly memorable team effort.

About the Author

DAN BERNSTEIN is a retired newspaper columnist and author of two picture books and *Justice in Plain Sight: How a Small-town Newspaper and its Unlikely Lawyer Opened America's Courtrooms.* He lives in Riverside, California, with his wife, Candia, and dogs, Sherman and Harry.

www.ingramcontent.com/pod-product-compliance
Lightning Source LLC
Chambersburg PA
CBHW040758120726
48005CB00012B/1232